Virtue
and
Vice

A Fascinating Journey into
Spiritual Transformation

By

Steven Craft

and

Roxon Flowers

Virtue and Vice

ISBN#: 1-59352-115-4

Unless otherwise noted, all quotations are from the King James Version of the Bible.

How to Contact Our Authors:

Rev. Steven L. Craft
E-mail: slcraft@veritasvalue.com

Mr. Roxon Flowers
E-mail: Rockyflowers@carolina.rr.com

Creative and publishing services by:

CSN Books Publishing
1975 Janich Ranch Court
El Cajon, CA 92019
Toll free: 866-484-6184
www.CSNbooks.com

INTRODUCTION

We met each other while attending Times Square Church, the church of Reverend David Wilkerson, author of *The Cross and the Switchblade*. Rocky's experiences as a New York City Police Officer, and Steven's experiences as a heroin addict and criminal (who eventually became a prison chaplain), make an incredible combination of experiences for a powerful and practical book.

When we teamed up to create *Virtue and Vice*, we quickly realized what an amazing story we had to tell, and how unique it was that God had brought us together to write it. Even though our lives were drastically different...Steven shooting illegal drugs, and Rocky enforcing the laws...our lives had many amazing parallels.

As you can well imagine, both of us have witnessed an abundance of *Virtue and Vice* in our own lives!

This book reflects our unique combination of unusual and exciting experiences, and shares the hard-earned spiritual truths we have learned from swimming in many of the cesspools of life.

In Rocky's case, he witnessed incredible hypocrisy on the police force, including poor moral leadership from the very top city officials. For example, one city official proudly rode in a New York City public parade...with his mistress at his side! And yes, he was still married at the time. That same top level city official spent money lavishly on city parties which were a severe waste of New York City funds.

As one of "New York City's finest," Rocky can personally testify as to how much the poor example of New York's top leadership impacted the attitude and moral fiber of the average cop on the New York City police force. "If top officials can do it," they would reason, "then why can't we do it?"

Virtue and Vice shares what we have learned through our own lives and experiences, and through observing the lives of others. We have come to understand that living a life that reflects a "double standard" comes with a very high price.

That is part of the warning and the wisdom in *Virtue and Vice*.

We honestly believe *Virtue and Vice* is the very first time when a long-term heroin addict and criminal (Rev. Craft), and a dedicated police officer (Rocky Flowers), have collaborated together to expose the contradictions and hypocrisies in our penal system, and, more importantly, in our own daily lives.

As you read about our experiences, we pray you will also reflect on your own ways of living life.

If your lifestyle somehow falls short of what you know it should be, we pray you will determine to raise up your life to a higher moral standard, deciding to choose virtue over vice.

Rev. Steven L. Craft
Ret. Detective Roxon Flowers

TABLE OF CONTENTS

Part Two

The Way to Virtue

Part Three

Undeserved, Unmerited Grace

PART ONE

Routine,
Reality,
Risk, and
Result

CHAPTER ONE

The Sorry Game

Worldly Sorrow Leads to Death

For godly sorrow produces repentance leading to salvation, not to be regretted; but the sorrow of the world produces death.
(2 Corinthians 7:10, NKJV)

Through the reality of our own lives, we have personally confirmed the truth found in the above Scripture. Godly repentance does direct and produce an attitude that leads and contributes to salvation and deliverance from evil.

Godly repentance never brings regret.

Worldly grief, the "hopeless sorrow," is characteristic of the pagan world, and, unfortunately, of a large portion of even Christian lives. Through trial and error, your authors have learned that this "worldly," shallow sorrow is destructive, ultimately ending in a spiritual, if not a literal, death. We will share from our personal testimonies concerning this conclusion as this book unfolds.

Here's how *The Living Bible* translates that same verse on repentance:

> *For God sometimes uses sorrow in our lives to help us turn away from sin and seek eternal life. We should never regret his sending it. But the sorrow of the man who is not a Christian is not the sorrow of true repentance and does not prevent eternal death.*
>
> (2 Corinthians 7:10, TLB)

THE FOUR R'S OF THE SORRY GAME

The first foundational truth we want to share with you in *Virtue and Vice* that we believe hinders change or true repentance is what we call "The sorry game" of the world. It functions through what we call the four R's:

Routine,
Reality,
Risk, and
Result.

As you will see conclusively as we share from our own experiences, this worldly sorrow ultimately leads to some form of death.

THE HABITUAL ROUTINE

The routine of worldly sorrow is habitual and continual sin, followed by a pathetic "I'm sorry" which has no lasting meaning. It is the "I'm sorry" of the abusive husband after he has battered his wife, then visits her in the hospital. A few days or weeks later, his lack of real sorrow results in yet another physical attack.

Habitual sinning and the subsequent sorrying (our own special word!) were frequently exemplified in both of our early lives.

Before Rocky gave his life to Christ in 1993, he had an emptiness that was reflected through a certain relationship in his past. He was living with a young lady; yet, he knew in his heart and mind that their relationship went against God's Word. Yet, because he desperately wanted to be involved with someone, he stayed in the *routine* of that sinful relationship.

As a result, there was a great deal of stress and strife involved in that union–the price paid for their sexual immorality. Virtually every time they engaged in any kind of fornication, Rocky would have strong feelings of regret, remorse, and even deep mourning within himself. Those pains of conscience lasted for about a week after each immoral sexual encounter.

It was a form of worldly *"sorrying."*

Ultimately, God showed Rocky that his fornicating lifestyle, outside of the sanctity of marriage, was a path to destruction and spiritual death. As long as he remained on that path, his relationship would fail to produce lasting pleasure or permanence.

Rocky's "sorrowing" was his feeling that "There is something wrong with this relationship." However, at the time of the relationship he was not quite capable of morally discerning what the "something wrong" was.

SORRYING ADDICTION

Steven Craft, unlike Rocky, was fortunate enough to be raised in a black Baptist church in the forties and fifties...at a time when virtually everyone seemed to be going to church (whether they were born-again Christians or not).

Yet, despite his church upbringing, Steven became a drug addict in 1964 after he left military service. He, unfortunately, became involved with a cousin in New York City who was a professional burglar and drug addict. This fellow lured Steven into heroin, where he remained hooked from 1964 until 1977—thirteen years of physical and mental hell!

During his addiction period, Steven would still go to church during the day, then shoot dope after the service. He was constantly seeking a "high" from various drugs, and when he sobered up, he would then cry out to God, asking the Lord to forgive him.

The next day, Steven's "sorrying" cycle would again repeat itself! That became his ugly, ungodly, self-destructive *routine.*

Steven experienced the habit of continual sinning, followed by the urgent plea to God for forgiveness. Steven's plea was really a self-deception that he was actually sorry for what he had done.

Sorrow without change is just an empty, useless emotion.

Real repentance involves change.

Steven cried out to God, "Lord, something is seriously wrong with my life. How can I actually believe You are forgiving me when I know in my heart that in a few days I'm actually going to do these same things again?"

Steven's habitual sin reflected his hypocrisy with God.

The habit produced constant sinning, getting high, and then trying to somehow pay penance in his human strength by running to church and "sorrying" at the altar...as if that particular place possessed some sort of spiritual magic or sacred answer.

EMPTINESS, HOPELESSNESS, AND CONTINUED SEARCHING

While Rocky was enmeshed in his immoral relationship, he was simultaneously reaching out to God
in the only way he knew how. "Lord, there must be
something better than what I'm experiencing right
now," he would pray.

Rocky received only temporary pleasure from the
relationship he was in, with no permanent fulfillment. He continued to sow his life into that destructive relationship. Every time he fornicated with his
young lady, he felt empty inside. Somehow he
instinctively understood that this relationship, as it
was constituted, would never result in true peace.
Marriage was not on the horizon, and Rocky had no
formal commitment to the woman involved.

Rocky constantly experienced a feeling of grieving
because somehow he knew he was going against
God's plan for his life (even though, at the time, he
was not familiar with the specifics of God's Word). He
grew up in a Protestant church where he was intro-
duced to religion by his grandmother. His experience
had little real meaning. He routinely occupied a
space in a pew on Sunday mornings, reluctantly lis-
tening to messages from God's Word that did not
seem to have much, if any, relevance to his young life.

THE CONSCIENCE WITHIN

Fortunately, God has set a small, stirring voice within each one of us that we have come to call a "conscience." This small voice faithfully alerts us when we do something that goes against His Holy Word. That's why, each time Rocky sinned in his relationship, the Holy Spirit helped him to know, deep down inside, that his lifestyle was not right or pleasing to God.

The more Rocky tried to stay with this woman, the more he felt less and less complete.

The more they engaged in sexual activities outside of wedlock, the more Rocky experienced a *deep saddening* within his own spirit, a deep knowing that his actions were somehow wrong.

Finally, Rocky reached a point in the relationship when he declared, "This relationship cannot go on." At that time, He cried out to the Lord, and suddenly his life started to come into a more godly focus.

DECEPTION AND STRUGGLE WITH SIN

Many Scriptures in God's Word deal with the subject of commitment...to God (our Creator), to our families, to our spouses, to our children, and to ourselves.

The Bible says,

Do not be deceived; God is not mocked: for

whatsoever a man soweth, that shall he also reap.

(Galatians 6:7, KJV)

In James 1:22, KJV, His Word declares:

But be doers of the word, and not hearers only, deceiving your own selves.

We both knew that we were trying to deceive ourselves about our sin. In our deception, we believed that by playing "the sorry game" we somehow were making an attempt at spiritual reform and a commitment to some sort of spiritual growth.

For Steven, the process was always the same.

1) Get high
2) Go to church and "repent"
3) Get high again

Steven repeated this pathetic three-part process over and over again, with no real commitment to change. Steven knew that his pattern was wrong, but he seemed absolutely powerless to stop it. Steven walked in the habit of sinning, followed by playing "the sorry game," followed by sinning again.

Of course, Steven wasn't really sorry. If he was, he would have stopped committing the sin. The fact that he kept repeating his sin clearly demonstrated that he was not really sorry at all.

Yet, every time he experienced this repeated worldly sorrow, he did feel bad. He sincerely *felt* like he was sorry. Steven's experience is what Paul describes in God's Word when he wrote:

> *For godly sorrow produces repentance leading to salvation, not to be regretted; but* <u>*the sorrow of the world produces death*</u>.
>
> (2 Corinthians 7:10, NKJV)
> (emphasis added by authors)

The Amplified Bible translates that passage in a slightly different way:

But <u>worldly grief</u> (the hopeless sorrow that is characteristic of the pagan world) <u>is deadly</u> [breeding and ending in death].

Steven struggled with drugs, while Rocky wallowed in sexual immorality. We both knew sin, and we both felt captive to a spirit of "hopeless sorrow" that bred an evil which ultimately could lead to death.

Neither of us could "see a way out."

We were held captive by an ungodly, habitual way of life.

CHAPTER TWO

Rocky's Reality:

Revelation for Change

Rocky understood that God had instituted marriage as a sanctioned covenant between a man and woman. Unfortunately, he had not digested enough of God's Word as a child to properly guide him as an adult. Instead of being governed by the Lord's compassionate and caring law, Rocky was a victim of his own set of worldly standards.

During the time period when Rocky was living a life of fornication, his *reality* was that "nothing seemed to go right."

Rocky shares here in his own words...

"In the world's eyes, I was doing fine. At the time I was working in a detective bureau doing investigations. I found myself getting deeper and deeper into my work, trying to escape the emptiness I was feeling inside."

Rocky tried to drown his sorrows and mask his emptiness through his work. As a result, he excelled in his police work by throwing himself passionately into each task or assignment. But while he was receiving high ratings and accolades in his department as an "excellent detective," his personal life and relationship with his lady reflected an empty, shallow mess.

"Each time I slept with this woman, I knew in my heart that it was wrong. I knew there had to be more to my life than this particular relationship."

At times, Rocky tried to share his feelings and stress with his lady companion, but she could not understand his frustration or emptiness. She had just come out of a marriage that ended in a divorce, so she was still grieving in her own spirit, and could not bring any real peace or depth to their relationship. Her own hurt hindered her ability to hear or help Rocky during the two years they remained together.

PERSONAL "REALITY"

The *reality* of Rocky's relationship was that he lived with a grieving lady who was experiencing the hurts and pains of divorce. Ironically, her life was mirroring the Scriptures even though she was not a

Christian. You see, when God spoke through the Apostle Paul, He essentially said, "The sorrow of the world, in the end, produces death."

Rocky's companion possessed a worldly streak and a worldly sorrow, so Satan successfully put a block in her spirit against a God-ordained marriage.

Her reality was that she was not open to think about God's plan for a man and a woman in the context of the marriage bond.

On the other hand, because of his smattering of a church background as a child, Rocky's reality could feel God dealing with his heart. Even though he, too, was lost at the time, the Holy Spirit was still drawing him to forsake sin and embrace righteousness.

You Cannot Hide from God

Rocky knew what he was doing was wrong, but he tried to hide his emptiness and sadness in his work. He continued to labor in the detective bureau...a very high stress job with high stress people. It was extremely difficult for him to try and suppress the emptiness inside, but he attempted to do so by drowning himself in the myriad of details in every criminal investigation.

Yet, everything he saw around him, instead of drowning out the shallowness, seemed to exacerbate it.

The more he sunk himself into his work, the more it appeared he was being productive. Yet, the harder he worked, the more the stress of the sinful home situation heightened, emphasizing the fact that the relationship was absolutely wrong.

Rocky began to stay away from the house more and more. At work, where he normally would put in ninety percent of his energy, he somehow found a way to channel a hundred and ten percent into his job.

The more he poured himself into his high stress job, the more evident it became to him that the world he was living in was simply a *reflection* of the world he saw in the police department...failed marriages, extramarital affairs, drinking, and drugs.

The issues he worked with daily in the police department – drugs, immorality, abuse, anger, etc. – were many of the same issues the police officers (including himself) were facing in his own department.

The appointed enforcers needed to be enforced!

Rocky increasingly tried to minimize his contacts with his lady at home in an attempt to avoid relationship issues which were ungodly, and, thus, ultimately doomed to fail.

God used this particular time to show Rocky that "You cannot run from Me."

At work, Rocky continued to encounter situations that exemplified what he was personally experiencing in his own life. He knew that since he was not married to this woman, in God's eyes he was doing something ungodly by engaging in fornication while living with that person out of wedlock.

One day he realized,

"I am doing the same stupid things that everyone else is doing in the society that I am appointed to serve and protect."

THE CLEAR CONFLICT

Many times Rocky would perform investigations involving unmarried couples who had entered into serious conflicts. Many had children in common, but were not married. Rocky would frequently wonder, "What kind of example is being set for the children when the father has not taken the responsibility to marry the woman of the house?"

Then, he would realize his own reluctance to marry his companion.

Rocky began to see that many of the problems that plague our society are because people were doing things that in God's eyes would grieve Him because they were morally wrong based upon the standards set forth in the Bible.

All day long he saw immorality. Yet, when he came home, Rocky would be forced to try and pretend that "things were just fine morally" in his own life.

"My situation is different," he would frequently rationalize to himself. "I know better than they do. I deal with these things on a daily basis, and see their errors, so everything is going to be fine for me and my lady."

But everything was not going to be fine!

Rocky began to realize that God was doing a work in him, helping him to discern that his feelings were not something the world could solve, or that this particular relationship could change. He began to see that "Me and the Lord are going to have to settle this alone."

CHASING THE TAIL

Prior to this particular relationship, Rocky had already started to feel an emptiness and futility inside. He felt the futility of a dog chasing its own tail, but never catching it. Others might view the dog chasing his tail as humorous, but to the dog, it is a deadly serious activity. "How many more times am I going to chase my own tail in an empty relationship?" he wondered. "When will I reach the point where I declare, 'Lord, I want to reach out to You'? I've got to cling to something greater than what I know right now."

Rocky's sense of satisfaction in his job began to decline.

His relationship at home was empty.

Step-by-step, Rocky began to understand that his emptiness could only be filled by the Lord. He started to seek for something beyond his own circumstances, beyond the things he could touch, beyond the man of worldly sorrow he was at the time.

CHAPTER THREE

Steven's Sense of Sorry and Routine

Because of his strong church background, Steven could skillfully play the sorry game better than most. He was a master at the *routine* of habitual sinning. He kept shooting heroin and smoking marijuana to experience a temporary ecstasy. When the drug high became an artificial low, Steven would then visit the local church, fall down on his knees at the altar, and tearfully confess his sin.

Again and again and again.

In some perverted way, his conscience became soothed whenever he visited the church after his getting high. Yet, like Rocky, he, too, felt more and more empty, experiencing a hollow spiritual shallowness.

However, unlike Rocky, Steven deceived himself into believing he was "really a good Christian" who just happened to be struggling with a weakness.

"God knows my heart and He understands me," he would reason. "No one else understands me, so no one else has the right to judge me."

Steven honestly believed he was "a man after God's own heart," and that God could take away his craving for drugs anytime <u>He</u> chose to do it. Since it hadn't yet happened, Steven mistakenly believed that "Maybe it just isn't God's time to heal me yet. When God is ready, He will get me off drugs one hundred percent," Steven would deceptively reason.

THE SHOOTING GALLERY MIRACLE

In the deepest part of his soul, Steven knew his logic was a lie, a shallow justification for his ungodly behavior. The devil tried desperately to convince Steven that his faulty logic was the real truth. Even Steven wanted to believe the lie because it made him feel better about himself...more comfortable.

The *reality* of that *routine*...habitual sin, followed by "the sorry game," followed by sin, created a void in his spirit.

One time Steven was with his cousin, "Jimmy the Weasel," a man who ultimately died of a drug overdose. Steven and Weasel were in a shooting gallery (where they mainlined dope) on 117th Street off of Lenox Avenue. Together they were shooting up very strong heroin from $3.00 bags.

Steven slowly felt himself going into a deep nod (like he was going into an overdose). He heard himself calling out in his spirit to God, "Lord, don't let me lose my life! Don't let me overdose."

Suddenly, the Spirit of God touched his spirit and brought him out of that deep nod!

After this life-saving experience, Steven immediately started to preach...right there in that shooting gallery! The Spirit of God had convicted him. Thankfully, the Word was already in him because he had grown up around the Word. Even though he had attended a dead, dry church, the Word of God is never dead.

> *So shall my word be that goeth forth out of my mouth: it shall not return unto me void, but it shall accomplish that which I please, and it shall prosper in the thing whereto I sent it.*
> (Isaiah 55:11, KJV)

The Word of God never returns void! It always accomplishes that for which it is sent. Even if the vessel who delivers the Word is corrupt (as Steven was), the Word itself is never corrupt!

Steven, nicknamed "Rev" by his fellow junkies, started preaching that day in the shooting gallery! The other junkies didn't quite know what to think. "That dope must really be good," they said, "because Rev's starting to quote the Word."

They even laughed.

But for Steven, his experience was very real.

Tears streamed down Rev's eyes as he preached while the needle was still in his arm; he watched the blood going up in that dropper. He pulled the needle out, and with blood trickling down, he continued to preach.

In his own spirit, Steven knew that it wasn't the drugs that made him preach. Yes, he was high, but it wasn't because of the dope. He was preaching because in his heart he had been touched by God, and he knew that shooting drugs was wrong. He knew clearly that he had no business there any longer. What he was doing was against God's will for his life.

Yet, Steven had no power to stop shooting drugs because of the routine of playing the sorry game. The constant saying of "I'm sorry" brought about a reality of spiritual shallowness in his heart. And now, as he was attempting to preach, he heard Satan screaming in his ear:

"You are a hypocrite. How dare you come and preach to these guys about Jesus Christ when you're in here doing the same thing. You're worse than they are."

Suddenly Steven stopped. Satan had a very good point. Satan's taunting placed a spiritual shallowness, an ungodly condemnation in him. He felt worthless and suddenly unable to share any more because he knew that what he was doing was wrong.

Steven left that shooting gallery feeling like a "Dr. Jekyll, Mr. Hyde." One part of him was a literal, walking dead man. Another part of him wanted to cry out to God so he could preach the Gospel in power and in truth to his fellow junkies.

Steven was caught between two worlds, suspended literally between heaven and hell.

There was no way out...except for the mercy of God.

THE SPIRITUAL PARALLELS

Even though Rocky's and Steven's situations were different from the world's eyes–Steven was an addict, Rocky was a policeman; spiritually, they were very similar and parallel.

Rocky tried to bury his pain in his work (his addiction), conducting intense criminal investigations with every ounce of his energy. Like Steven, he too heard the accusations from Satan.

"You are a bigger criminal than those you arrest," the enemy would say. "You are a hypocrite. They are not trying to be something they aren't. But you, with your badge, are living in sin; yet, you are trying to act all righteous. How can you have the audacity to make arrests on domestic violence cases when your own home situation is so bad, full of tension and arguments? You are hiding your sins behind your badge."

We both were starting to clearly understand what Paul meant when he wrote that worldly sorrow breeds and leads to death. In our cases, the worldly sorrow, if not changed, would lead to spiritual death, and, ultimately, eternal death. In Steven's case, it could also soon lead to a literal death.

We were beginning to realize that the issue of virtue and vice was deadly. We had to somehow end the routine of our habitual sin, followed by the false, repentant spirit of "the sorry game."

Ultimately, this habitual routine of sin was leading us down a pathetic path of becoming spiritually hard and shallow.

CHAPTER FOUR

Assessing the Risks

In this chapter, we want to look at some of the risks involved in living the routine and the reality of "the sin and sorry game."

Risk One:
A hardening or a loss of spiritual sensitivity

In Rocky's life as a New York City police detective who was living in a sexual sinful relationship, he experienced a hardening of his spiritual sensitivity.

That hardening started because of the type of career he had selected. As a police officer, Rocky was formally trained to stuff his feelings into his back pocket. To be effective as a police officer, he was instructed to stifle his emotions when confronted with scenes such as a shooting, or a life-or-death encounter. A police officer, by virtue of the many different scenarios he/she encounters, must be trained to take thoughts, desires, and feelings and void them completely out in order to be effective in the various job encounters.

Rocky was trained, as a police officer, to stifle feelings and desires. Unfortunately, as so many in the profession ultimately do, he took that professional practice of stoicism and brought it into his personal relationship.

How could Rocky possibly come home and share how he was displeased with the kind of relationship he had when both his and her police training fostered that very kind of relationship?

Rocky performed at work void of feeling, trained to not be sensitive, no matter what foul language or unkind gestures he encountered. The insensitivity and desensitization he experienced so completely at work on any given day now started to permeate his personal relationship.

Rocky's young lady was also in the same vocation and had been trained the same way! So, rather than growing to the level where they were able to communicate in an open, honest relationship, they were both basically suppressing the thoughts and feelings they were experiencing.

Sensitivity had been deadened.

Rocky's job indoctrinated him into the kind of lifestyle where it was commonplace to bring the problems on the job home (despite what many police personnel might tell you!). If there isn't another avenue in which to dissipate that stuff – such as alcohol, drugs, or some other extra-curricular outlet such as pornography or extra-marital affairs...you bring it home.

Rocky was living in a sinful relationship as his addiction, but reasoned, "You know what, it's okay. We are two consenting adults, and this works for us."

Questions of morality were not relevant.

Because the young lady was also a police officer, her own spirit and conscience had been seared. Further, she was struggling with many issues from failed, past relationships. It was almost like there was an impenetrable wall, a great gulf, that existed between them. There was no way they could come home from their jobs and even begin to try and talk about important relationship issues.

Both had learned how to keep their defenses up and project a strong front. Rocky's lady had learned to manifest the character of a self-made, liberated woman who really didn't need any man.

That relationship was doomed for failure because the Lord wasn't in it.

A relationship that played the game of habitual sinning, followed by "the sorry game," followed by new sinning, followed by "the sorry game," could only produce a hallow reality of spiritual shallowness.

Their hearts were hardened; their spirits were desensitized; their spiritual consciousness was numb.

That inner voice in Rocky that said, "Hey, this is wrong. I've got to get out of this situation while I still can," grew weaker and weaker as his heart grew harder and harder.

DRUG ADDICTION DEADENS

Steven was experiencing similar emotions in the context of his own sin, drug addiction. Drugs desensitize one's mind and one's spirit. A desperate junkie will literally kill his mother for a shot of dope. There is nothing an addict won't do. That's why there are always an abundance of young girls on the street, selling their bodies, even though they know they are susceptible to numerous sexual diseases. Drugs drive them.

There are far too many documented cases of the demon addiction. In one recent case, an addict went into a bar, enticed a middle-class woman to drink too much, invited her into his car, then drove her to the country where he put a belt around her neck, pulled her around the car on the ground and through the bushes. Ultimately, he raped her and then tried to murder her. But by the grace of God, a person delivering early morning newspapers spotted the man dragging the lady out the car with his belt around her neck. He called the police on his cell phone, and just in a nick of time the police officers caught and busted this addict before he had a chance to kill the lady.

It turns out this man was already a murderer from thirty years ago, and a previous rapist, but had only received a small amount of time, and was now out on parole. Hopefully, this time he will be locked up for good. His case clearly demonstrates that there is absolutely nothing an addict won't do!

HARDENED HEARTS

It is amazing how our hearts can become so hardened and dead. If we continue in habitual sin, we will experience a hardened heart, and after awhile, little in life will move or touch you.

When the police busted the rapist in the story I just shared, he was ready to strangle this girl whom he had just raped. The newspaper reported that the man was so driven by lust that he tossed open his car door, put the belt around her neck, and pulled her through the dirt and bushes by her neck! And, if that newspaper delivery person had not "just happened" (divine coincidence?) to be going by, and witnessed this tragic incident at about three o'clock in the morning, that lady would be dead now.

When Rev. Craft heard about this incident, he wondered, "Will this girl now give her life to the Lord, realizing that it was only the great mercy of God that saved her life?"

Of course, the reporters gave no glory to God, instead reporting that the lady "was lucky" that the man happened to be passing by on his paper route.

We share this example to make this one simple point as clear as we can make it: sin results in a deep hardening of any spiritual sensitivity, and bit-by-bit, if unchecked, that sin and insensitivity will lead to human extremes such as rape and murder.

In Rev. Craft's case, the more dope he shot, the harder his heart became.

The more deceived he was, the more mistakenly convinced he was that God somehow understood that he was simply a disobedient rebel.

Only later would Steven fully understand how heroin had become his god.

In his own sinful mind, Steven was convinced that nobody could judge him. He foolishly reasoned, "God has the power, because He's God, to take this desire for heroin out of my mind anytime He wants to. Since He hasn't done so yet, He isn't ready for me to get sober. He will do it as soon as He is ready."

That perverted logic is yet another vivid illustration of the deception of sinfulness! Steven had actually rationalized that God had the power to free him, and since He hadn't done it yet, then it must be God's will that he remain an addict for a while longer!

The Bible speaks about the deceitfulness of sin.

But exhort one another daily, while it is called

*today; lest any of you be hardened through the
deceitfulness of sin.*

(Hebrews 3:13)

Risk Two:
Spiritual and Emotional Slavery

Sin so deceived Steven that drugs became harder
and harder to resist. He would mainline, all the while
believing the lie that God was not yet ready to heal
him from his addiction. Steven entered into a heavy
spiritual slavery brought about through this risk,
through this reality and routine of the sorry game.

Heavy spiritual slavery brings you to one end: you
are locked in chains to the bondage of sin.

Rocky and Steven both experienced a hardening,
and insensitivity that made them slaves to their sins
and their circumstances.

Once Rocky thought about trying to resolve some
of the issues in his relationship by attending a church
that his lady's mother had recommended, and was
attending. On one particular Sunday Rocky and his
lady went to a neighborhood Baptist church in the
hopes of somehow reducing some of the tremendous
stress in their relationship, and at work.

Both Rocky and his lady felt that they would forever be slaves to this relationship. Rocky sat in the
church, but was not familiar with the mechanics of
this particular denomination. When a song was being

sung by one of the choir members, he wasn't sure whether to stand or sit. He felt overwhelmed and awkward, in an environment where he was not the one exercising the control.

Suddenly, he began grieving and weeping uncontrollably. He knew he had reached some sort of breaking point, and that he was involved in some sort of slavery. He knew that the only way he could experience or get beyond this was to allow the Lord to do something.

Rocky could no longer cope with the entire sin/sorrow cycle. He was weary of the emptiness, the shallowness, the lack of sensitivity.

He cried uncontrollably in excess of ten minutes.

"I could not grasp exactly what God was doing in me and through me, but my heart felt like it was about to explode."

It wasn't until that particular incident happened that Rocky began to realize that he would be forever doomed if he tried to stay in that sinful relationship.

There had to be a way out.

Rocky started looking beyond his circumstances, beyond his situation. In his own spirit, and in his own way, he started looking beyond all he had previously known.

He was clear on one point: his current relationship, his current companion brought no solace, no communication, no fulfillment. Nothing about that particular relationship gave him any kind of lasting satisfaction.

Rocky was a spiritual slave...because his relationship was outside of the sacred sacrament of matrimony that God instituted for man and woman. His current relationship was forever doomed since his sin left a place, an opening for the enemy to come in and attack the two of them.

As a police officer, Rocky had constant access to women on a daily basis. He was exposed to women of all ages, creeds, colors, and professions. So, he knew that there could be much more to a relationship, and he wanted to have a deeper relationship...one that God could bless.

CHAPTER FIVE

Spiritual Slavery and Bondage

People today frequently discuss the issue of slavery from a physical or a cultural context, especially in the African-American community. They especially talk about the time in American history when slavery was legal, rightfully moaning and groaning about how despicable slavery was for our country.

And they are right.

But most do not fully grasp that even though their black forefathers were *physical* slaves, many of them were also Christians while they were in physical slavery. And black history (yes, much has been expunged!) writes about the spirituals that the slaves sung, writes about the hope of the slaves who lived in Jesus Christ. In fact, it is said that during slavery their most blessed time was Sunday when the slave-master would allow them to hold church in the field. For those few hours they were spiritually free, and even though their physical bodies were still in bondage.

Today, the slavery we are writing about here is of the soul, not the body.

The *routine* of habitual sinning and sorrying produces the *reality* of spiritual shallowness which then is followed by the risk of the hardening of the heart and spiritual insensitivity, which then *results* in a heavy spiritual slavery far more devastating than any physical slavery known to man!

Why?

This slavery is bound by invisible, spiritual chains that do not wrap around your body, but around the mind and spirit of man, and go with him wherever he goes, and are with him in every situation.

Steven's addictions produced spiritual bondage; he became a spiritual slave to heroin. When he would enter into a drug program, he did not benefit from the program because even when he was sitting in the encounter groups, he would just go through the motions asked of him. But always, in the back of his mind, he was thinking about the first chance he would have to go out into the community and get another shot of dope!

That's slavery.

Steven was obsessed with the idea of getting high again, and his bondage was complete.

Heroin was his god.

He was literally guilty of the commandment,

Thou shalt have no other gods before me. Thou shalt not make unto thee any graven image, or any likeness of any thing that is in heaven above, or that is in the earth beneath, or that is in the water under the earth:
(Exodus 20: 3-4, KJV)

Steven's graven image – emblazed upon his imagination – was the white powder, heroin, which consumed and obsessed his thinking!

Steven did not think about Jesus Christ. The only time he would think about godly things was when he was afraid of dying. He possessed a false, worldly sorrow that led to death.

WORTHLESS TEARS WITH NO WAY OUT

Rocky shed tears in church that day, but he left that day and went back to his house where he continued to sin, cry, sin again, then play "the sorry game." Just as Steven, he remained in bondage due to a habitual sin, followed by sorrying which led to a hardened heart.

We were both living examples of our primary text:

For godly grief and the pain God is permitted to direct, produce a repentance that leads and contributes to salvation and deliverance from evil, and it never brings regret; but worldly grief (the hopeless sorrow that is characteristic

*of the pagan world) is deadly [breeding and
ending in death].*

(2 Corinthians 7:10 AMP)

We were simply reflections of our society where
so many cry out, "It's hopeless. There's no way out."

Millions upon millions upon millions of people are
caught up in this cycle of sin and slavery.

Hopelessness is the main reason why suicide rates
in this country have skyrocketed and drug addiction
rates have ballooned. Alcoholism is pervasive, and
sex crimes are as prolific as the Internet porno sites.

HOPELESS WITHOUT CHRIST

From our cold, hard experiences over the years, we
have come to the conclusion that without Jesus
Christ, worldly sorrow will continue to go on.

Without Jesus, the habitual sinning and the feeling sorry later will continue. The shallowness will
always be there because there cannot be any depth or
satisfaction to anything that you are doing right now
that is outside of God's rules.

Your sensitivity will diminish.

You will become desensitized to the acts you are
committing, and the things you continue to do will
grow more and more vile. At some point, you will
become a slave to whatever is the sinful habit.

Rocky concluded his police career in the vice unit where he continuously saw firsthand the impact of the sin cycle. Only after Rocky made the decision to give his life to Christ did he begin to see how entrenched he was in sinful behavior.

Only God and God alone could shed real light on his life and break the bondage he was in!

When Rocky started to see things as a Christian, he realized that "In my vice experience, my fellow workers were experiencing the same habits, the same sins, the same methods, the same ugly experiences as those they were busting."

He saw in them the different phases of "the sorry game," and grew to realize that "Until you come to a saving knowledge of Christ, until the veil is removed from your face and your eyes, you will never clearly see the spiritual dimension."

You will never be able to walk away from "the sorry game" without the Holy Spirit convicting you, bringing you through your journey of life. The Holy Spirit will give you wisdom, and then you will begin to discern what is morally wrong and what goes against God's laws and rules.

That kind of conviction can only come from surrendering your life to the Lord Jesus Christ!

Without God, the game is a perpetual cycle of sin.

CHAPTER SIX

Domestic Violence and Other Sin Cycles

Rocky saw the cycle of sin and sorrying mirrored in the cases he handled involving domestic violence.

"In the beginning, there is a love phase. Then there's something in between that phase that brings the batterer to the point where he is either not happy, or starts to move into the second phase where he's battering. He moves into the battering phase whether the battered individual has done anything or not. He will always find an excuse to batter. After the attack, the batterer then enters into the phase where he proclaims 'I am sorry for my actions,' although he usually tries to justify the beating. 'Yes, I'm sorry I hit you, but you shouldn't have burnt my eggs.'"

"Next comes reconciliation. The batterer makes contrite concessions to the victim to try and make amends for what he has done to his spouse. Then, the phases start all over again!"

Society has proven it is powerless to institute changes or solve the myriad of moral problems that rock our country. Both of us have worked in law enforcement in different capacities, and sad to say, we see no signs that crime will ever be prevented or reduced to any significant degree. Despite great technological breakthroughs to catch criminals, there has been little breakthrough in the way of changing human behavior to motivate criminals to live right.

So society continues to flourish in the pattern of "the sorry game."

"I'm sorry that I busted your eye last night, baby, but you shouldn't have made me mad when I was tired. You shouldn't have started to nag me because the bills weren't paid. You made me go off on you. Forgive me. I apologize for the black eye. Hey, let me go down to the store and buy you some new, dark glasses."

That's the web of habitual sinning and sorrying.

In the same example, a few days later another trigger will pop up as the victim touches one of his billion hot buttons, and he blackens her other eye. This cycle goes on and on until the batterer becomes totally insensitive and hardened.

Over the long term, the batterer sometimes causes the one being battered to ultimately become a batterer. At some point she thinks to herself, "I'm going to kill him in his sleep tonight because I'm tired of him beating on me." Next comes the murder case after she puts a knife in his head in the middle of the night while he is sleeping.

These types of murders committed by women are the result of the Battered Women's Syndrome.

"The sorry game" usually ends up in some sort of death. Death of self. Death of spirit. Death of soul. And sometimes, a literal death.

PATTERNED SIN CYCLES

The same sin cycle, the same pattern repeats itself with drugs, alcohol, pornography, or any other addiction.

Domestic violence is just one example of the sin, the sorrow, the determination to do better, followed by the sin and more sorrow. The cycle is never-ending, and as we have seen throughout Part One of this book, worldly sorrow breeds and ends in death.

Rocky, as a police officer saw cases where death literally was the product of the battered women syndrome. There are many women sitting in state penitentiaries right now because they refused to suffer the beatings any longer, deciding to murder the men who battered them.

In the area of pornography, the very same problems manifests itself: a routine, a reality, a risk, and a result. With each act, there is a gradual escalation in the attempts to discover forbidden pleasure. A married man looking at sexy photos on the Internet will eventually find the need to "graduate" to real, live "escorts" who will service his sexual fantasies.

Sex crimes contain the same invisible chains of bondage, and the products of sexual perversion are, unfortunately, manifested outside and inside of law enforcement.

No one is exempt from the game! Only our Lord and Savior Jesus Christ can break the slavery.

There was a young man Rocky worked with in the vice unit. In the police department's eyes, this young man was an excellent detective, an excellent undercover officer. But, deep in his heart, he was caught up in the lifestyle of pornography due to the temptations he experienced on a day-to-day basis.

The experiences he gained in the vice unit gave him an overwhelming feeling that he was invincible, sort of a "superman" who could do whatever he wanted without getting caught. This false sense of euphoria led him to become bolder and more careless.

On one of his days off, this young man went to an area noted for picking up prostitutes. He decided that he was going to capitalize on his vice experience, and the fact that he was a police officer. This individual picked up a known prostitute and made an agreement to have a sex act performed on him. At some point, in the middle of the act, he became violent and assaulted the young lady. He tossed her naked out of his car and drove off. The victim then flagged down a marked police car and explained all that had occurred. Subsequently, the police car located this off-duty officer a few blocks away where he had become involved in an accident in the middle of an intersection.

The young police officer was arrested. Instead of protecting what he was sworn to uphold, he had exploited this young lady. The very laws he put people in jail for he was trying to circumvent for his own lusts and desires. That young police officer ended up doing time in prison. He broke the very laws he swore to uphold. While pledging to protect others, he violated the laws himself.

In another instance, a young officer was called upon, in an undercover capacity, to go into houses of prostitution. This young man was given the job because his superiors believed he could go into the house, make the necessary deal with the prostitute, and then make the arrest. They were confident he would not go beyond the scope of his job and circumvent the law.

In a vice unit, officers are instructed to undress only down to the underwear. To institute an arrest, the officer only needs an agreement and an offer...not the actual sex act. Once there's an agreement and an offer, an arrest can be made. But, this particular young officer, even though carefully trained and screened, decided to go through with the act. Of course, he was subsequently reprimanded, and received stern disciplinary action from the police department.

STRONGLY ENTRENCHED SIN

Pornography in our society is strongly entrenched. We see it on television, in commercials, and glorified in movies, sports, and magazines, including the mainstream *Sports Illustrated* swimsuit issue. Pornography, if you are not careful, is a powerful tool that the enemy will use to keep you in bondage.

Our bodies are a sacred thing, created by God for mutual pleasure in a marriage relationship. God's Word warns us about seeking a momentary euphoria by fornicating with someone, or by having sexual intercourse outside of the sacrament of marriage.

Sexual sins are clearly forbidden!

> *But I say unto you, That whosoever looketh on a woman to lust after her hath committed adultery with her already in his heart.*
> (Matthew 5:28)

As we supposedly "progress" in our society, one does not have to look very far to see that there is one crime statistic that has not changed – sex crimes!

In the last decade, there has been great praise for government officials and police departments for supposedly reducing crime. But, if we look at the statistics closely, if we trace them back five or ten years, the one area that has not been impacted is in the area of sex crimes. The enemy uses sex crimes to keep our society in bondage, to make us believe the lie that, "My body is my own and I can do with it what I please. When there are two consenting adults, then whatever they decide to do together sexually is just fine."

But that's not the way God instituted the relationship between a man and a woman.

THE LINGERING HYPOCRISY

It has never ceased to amaze us how, when we talk about these issues of *Virtue and Vice* to others, how deep the hypocrisy goes. For example, as a society we strongly condemn sexual crimes, especially rape, incest, and prostitution. Legislatures have pain- stakingly set up laws and statutes against these crimes, making them felonies. Specialized police units called "vice squads" and "special victims units" exist to defeat these sexual offenses.

Yet, our society openly promotes the very material that fuels these offenses in the first place: namely, pornography and illicit behavior (lasciviousness, as the Bible calls it).

How can we, with one side of our mouths, condemn these practices, and in the next breath put out pornographic material glorifying rape?

It is hypocrisy at it's highest level!

Our laws, whether or not we choose to acknowledge it, were based on God's principles and on the Ten Commandments. If you trace the history of our laws, they were handed down clearly through the Scriptures.

The amazing contradiction is in the fact that those who are called to uphold these laws are themselves engaging in these kinds of activities, hiding behind a badge, saying, "As long as there are two consenting adults, it's okay."

The depth of this hypocrisy is almost beyond anyone's imagination!

From 1995 through 1997, Rocky worked in a "special victims" unit where he made arrests of men (usually over the age of 21) who were having sexual intercourse with underage women. He was sworn to make these arrests and to uphold the law that basically said, "A young lady below age 18 cannot engage in any kind of permissible sexual intercourse with a man over the age of 21 years of age."

In contrast to this law, and to demonstrate the hypocrisy of our society, pornographic magazines and web sites on the Internet freely show adults having intercourse and conducting perverted acts with "barely legal" girls dressed up to look like young children, or in the most perverted sites, men having sex with children. Society tries to defend this sin by calling it "an expression of our First Amendment rights that should not be censored."

How does law enforcement uphold these laws when they are constantly running into moral conflicts and contrary signs from the society as a whole?

Have you noticed that there is nothing sacred on television anymore? It is common during the most popular viewing hours to see simulated sexual acts on television. And, what God has called an abomination – the homosexual explosion – is purposely being promoted to expose their lifestyle to the masses.

> *And likewise also the men, leaving the natural use of the woman, burned in their lust one toward another; men with men working that which is unseemly, and receiving in themselves that recompense of their error which was meet.*
>
> (Romans 1:27, KJV)

Pornography and homosexuality are tools Satan is using to hook our society into sin.

By giving condoms to our youth, we are clearly saying, "It's okay to have sex before you get married. Go ahead, enjoy yourself!" We are fostering habits of immoral sex in our youth by telling them, "If you have some feeling for each other, or if you just want to experiment, go ahead and have intercourse! Just use a condom." That habit breeds multiple partners. It is only later on in adulthood when the young ladies start to realize that their bodies were impacted by these random sexual acts which occurred long before they were spiritually, mentally, or physically ready. Many end up with unwanted pregnancies or diseases.

Later on, they bear unwanted and unplanned children, and their bodies undergo needless trauma all because of the immoral teachings, the deceptive, misleading concepts that were placed in their heads by our society when they were too young to filter and judge for themselves.

Clearly, pornography not only desensitizes adults, but it is now permeating the lives of our children. Go into almost any convenience store and there are openly pornographic magazines within the reach of children. Any child can go on the Internet and pull up pornography within a few minutes, even if the computer they are on supposedly has "filters" to protect them from such filth.

THE PROOF IN PRISON

Reverend Craft has spent years as a chaplain in the prison system, and one thing is abundantly clear from those experiences: pedophiles, rapists, and sexual offenders all started out by being lured into the web of pornography. They were exposed to it at some level. Some were the victims of a sexual assault as a child. Others developed a sexual habit because some adult told them when they were children that sex and pornography were just fine, and in many cases, those adults made the pornography available to them.

So the habit developed. The child always knew, in their own mind, that the sin was wrong, and they had a sorrow in their hearts, but had no way of expressing it because they trusted the adult who was perpetuating this vile act on them. The child then grew up and became desensitized to these pornographic acts, and, subsequently, fell into spiritual slavery.

In the vice squad Rocky met many young ladies who he had to personally lock up for prostitution. Most of them have been exposed to some kind of sexual act that was perpetuated on them at a very early age. Sex then became a habit. They were sexually abused so regularly that eventually they became desensitized to it.

Then the sexual slavery became a means to an end. They learned that they could sell their bodies, even though they knew it was possible that they could lose their lives by picking up a "John" that was a potential murderer, or by contracting a deadly sexual disease.

Yet, they continue to prostitute themselves! Some have been raped, some assaulted, some shot, but they continue to do this.

Why?

They continue to engage in these sexually perverse acts because they have become desensitized. They have become slaves to their sexual behavior. Pornography and sexual perversion are always the starting points for the beginning of what will eventually become sexual slavery.

WHY DO WE PROMOTE SIN?

Steven, as a former heroin addict, personally experienced how drugs and alcohol were destructive 30 years ago. The evidence is overwhelming! Yet, today alcohol and drugs are increasingly and constantly promoted through the media, entertainment, and even through sports, as a pleasurable part of the "good life" experience.

Society promotes drug abuse, alcohol abuse, pimping, prostitution, and crime as a profitable, exciting lifestyle, but with only one caution: "Just don't get caught. Go for the gusto. Shoot all the dope you can, drink at all the parties you can, rape all the women you can, have all the homosexual experiences you can. Gay is good, dope is good, alcohol is good. Be a guzzler. Do whatever turns you on. If it feels good, do it. Just don't get caught, because if you do, the laws say you will receive a punishment."

Drink and drive...just don't get caught.

Have sex with prostitutes...just don't let your wife find out.

Party until you drop...but don't make so much noise that your neighbor calls the police.

The new-style pornographer can sit down in the privacy of his own home, turn on his computer, then look at a seemingly endless progression of vile images. He can watch old men having sex with animals, or, if he is in one of the "special clubs," he can watch old men have sex with children.

That sexual madness permeates the man's life; yet, we have the audacity to actually act offended and shocked beyond belief when that same man turns off his computer and goes out to engage in these same sins.

Wake up America!

Day in and day out sex crimes are committed on our streets because these men have been viewing vile images on the Internet.

Yet, we act like we don't know what to do.

We feebly claim it is these offenders "First Amendment rights" to look at this stuff.

So we feign surprise.

"Oh, did you hear what happened in South Philly last night? A woman was snatched out of a bar, tossed in a car, taken out into the country, and brutally raped and strangled. The perpetrator of this dastardly crime must be caught."

Wait a minute!

The very detective declaring that the perpetrator must be caught could be a pervert himself, privately watching pornography on his home computer.

The Bible foretells a time such of this.

> *Woe unto them that call evil good, and good evil; that put darkness for light, and light for darkness; that put bitter for sweet, and sweet for bitter!*
>
> (Isaiah 5:20, KJV)

On one hand; our society promotes wickedness, and, on the other, we penalize people for practicing what it is we are promoting!

When are we going to recognize the obvious?

The sin game leads to the routine of habitually doing evil. These people are then caught, and put in jail, for doing the very evil society promotes.

Habitual sin brings about a reality of hollowness, of falseness, of hypocrisy, and shallowness.

How can we keep coming against criminals for committing crimes that we, as a society, have tempted them to commit?

We are trying to have it, literally, both ways in the area of crime and criminality.

Crime is both glorified and vilified in America.

Which way is it?

Do we want virtue or vice?

We can't have both!

CHAPTER SEVEN

Rise Up, America!

We believe it is time to clean up the television industry, the media, the libraries, to tell people that sin is wrong, and stigmatize those who perpetrate sin upon our society.

It is time to stop allowing vile garbage to pollute our children's minds. We must rise up and show our hatred and displeasure for the sexual sins that are destroying the very moral fabric of our lives.

America must rise up...or, America must decide to totally open the immoral floodgates and allow everybody to do whatever they want to do whenever they want to do it, and as much as they want to do it.

That is really the critical choice we face.

America could open up the penitentiaries and let the criminals pour out, deciding to ignore sex crimes and statutes, and forget about sex offender registries. If that sounds bizarre, let us ask you this question:

"Why do we register sex offenders and then allow them personal access to a personal computer where there are literally thousands of websites that portray the very acts they are charged not to commit?"

Does anyone else out there feel this process is madness?

We have heard it said, "Criminals don't change."

How can they?

They are being given mixed messages by our society; our "criminals" merely are a mirror reflection of a society in bondage to heavy spiritual slavery (this indictment includes many of the people in law enforcement who are appointed to enforce the laws).

ABOVE THE LAW?

The laws declare that we cannot commit illicit acts of prostitution, rape, etc.; yet, law-enforcement personnel are, in fact, doing these very same things themselves, and normally, with little or no repercussions or accountability.

You have probably heard the expression, "No one is above the law."

But in your own community, do you really believe that? Do you believe the law enforcement personnel are treated in the same way as the regular citizens?

When was the last time a policeman received a ticket from a fellow policeman?

In fact, the very ones who write the laws and who are supposed to uphold the laws are frequently those doing the same things as the people they are arresting. The only difference: the police personnel are doing it with no penalties.

The more accurate statement for our society seems to be, "Do what you've got to do, but just don't get caught doing it."

BEYOND HABITUAL SIN

At the beginning of this section, we quoted the Apostle Paul:

> *But worldly grief, the hopeless sorrow that is characteristic of the pagan world, is deadly, breeds and ends in death.*
> (2 Corinthians 7:10, AMP)

The Living Bible translates 2 Corinthians 7:10 as follows:

> *For God sometimes uses sorrow in our lives to help us turn away from sin and seek eternal life.*

We should never regret His sending sorrow, but the sorrow of man who is not a Christian is not the sorrow of true repentance and it does not prevent eternal death.

We believe that our society will never be able to see beyond habitual sin until we acknowledge God for whom He is – the Creator of the universe. We must collectively recognize that He is The Law-maker who has set down a moral standard for us to follow.

Without these acknowledgements, worldly sorrow will continue.

Habitual sinning, and feeling sorry later on, will continue.

Our society will ultimately reach new depths of shallowness. Spiritual sensitivity will diminish, and, ultimately, harden in every aspect of our culture and our lives.

The moral pervasive permissiveness is all around us.

Parents buy revealing (they consider it flattering) clothing for their young daughters, and think it is cute and harmless when they look "sexy."

Fathers encourage their sons to engage in sexual intercourse with the local high school prom queen or cheerleader, boasting that their son is a "man," "a stud," or has "a way with the gals."

The message being sent out to our nation and our youth is, "Go ahead and do it. It's okay. Just don't get caught. Don't get pregnant. Don't catch AIDS or STDS (sexually transmitted diseases)."

God's moral law declares that marriage was created for a man and a woman (who would have ever thought we would need to state it that way?), and that sexual intercourse is intended to be within the confines of marriage.

> *Therefore shall a man leave his father and his mother, and shall cleave unto his wife: and they shall be one flesh.*
>
> (Genesis 2:24 KJV)

Unfortunately, the immoral sexual behavior we see in our "criminals" is simply a mirror reflection of that behavior of our society as a whole. The "criminals" just get caught.

CONFLICT AND CONTRADICTION

How can we possibly continue to uphold our laws in earnest when we, as a society, continue to break those laws ourselves?

Vice permeates the very fabric of America.

As we close Part One of our book, we would like to give you a brief understanding of what we call "God's moral law."

Simply stated, that law is the Ten Commandments which God gave to Moses for the children of Israel on Mount Sinai when He brought the children of Israel (the Jews) out of Egyptian slavery.

The early Jews were in a literal slavery; today, we are the spiritual Jews, and we, too, are in a spiritual slavery. The Ten Commandments are our only hope for breaking the bondage we are in. God declared these ten laws in Chapter Twenty of Exodus for our well-being, and for the prosperity of society.

And God spake all these words, saying, I am the LORD thy God, which have brought thee out of the land of Egypt, out of the house of bondage.

Thou shalt have no other gods before me.

Thou shalt not make unto thee any graven image, or any likeness of any thing that is in heaven above, or that is in the earth beneath, or that is in the water under the earth:

Thou shalt not bow down thyself to them, nor serve them: for I the LORD thy God am a jealous God, visiting the iniquity of the fathers upon the children unto the third and fourth generation of them that hate me;

And shewing mercy unto thousands of them that love me, and keep my commandments.

Thou shalt not take the name of the LORD thy God in vain; for the LORD will not hold him guiltless that taketh his name in vain.

Remember the Sabbath day, to keep it holy.

Six days shalt thou labour, and do all thy work:

But the seventh day is the Sabbath of the LORD thy God: in it thou shalt not do any work, thou, nor thy son, nor thy daughter, thy manservant, nor thy maidservant, nor thy cattle, nor thy stranger that is within thy gates:

For in six days the LORD made heaven and earth, the sea, and all that in them is, and rested the seventh day: wherefore the LORD blessed the Sabbath day, and hallowed it.

Honour thy father and thy mother: that thy days may be long upon the land which the LORD thy God giveth thee.

Thou shalt not kill.

Thou shalt not commit adultery.

Thou shalt not steal.

Thou shalt not bear false witness against thy neighbour.

Thou shalt not covet thy neighbour's house, thou shalt not covet thy neighbour's wife, nor his manservant, nor his maidservant, nor his ox, nor his ass, nor any thing that is thy neighbour's.

(Exodus 20:1-17, KJV)

In Part Two of our book, we will share how, with God's Law as our solid foundation, our society (any society) can move out from the muck and the mire of spiritual slavery (which comes from ignoring God's commandments), and begin to walk in a life of hope and virtue.

Part Two

The Way
to Virtue

CHAPTER EIGHT

How to End the Sorry Game

What will bring us out of "the sorry game?"

What "wake-up call" does it take?

What events will break that never ending cycle of habitual sinning and sorrowing that leads to spiritual, eternal and physical death?

> *For godly grief and the pain God has permitted to direct produces a repentance that leads and contributes to salvation and deliverance from evil and it never brings regret.*
>
> (2 Corinthians 7:10, AMP)

The NIV translation reads,

> *Godly sorrow brings repentance that leads to salvation and leaves no regret.*

Grief comes from godly sorrow which leads to repentance. The Bible uses the Greek word "metanoia" for "repentance," meaning "a change of mind." The Bible warns us that unless we repent, or change our minds, we will all "likewise perish."

Most amazingly, these are the words of Jesus Christ Himself!

John the Baptist preached repentance in the wilderness. He declared, "Repent, for the kingdom of God is at hand."

Repentance is primary.

Without godly repentance, there can be no salvation or deliverance.

THE TOUGH QUESTIONS

Understanding the importance of repentance, we still need to ask two tough questions:

1) "Where does repentance originate?"
2) "What is the source of this changed mind?"

The source is godly grief.

Worldly thinking says, "I'm sorry I got caught and now I have to pay the piper."

Godly sorrow says, "I am wrong, and I am sorry I have offended and sinned against God, my Creator."

Godly grief arises from the ownership of our sins.

When Rev. Craft was a drug addict, he played the old "sorry game." He deceptively believed a lie.

"God knows my heart," he would declare, "and He knows that I love Him. God knows I struggle with dope, that I'm weak, that my spirit is indeed willing but my flesh is weak. God can take away from me this desire for drugs whenever He wants to."

What Rev. Craft did not understand was that the spirit of sin he inherited from his spiritual forefather, Adam, was the same attitude Adam had when God confronted him in the Garden of Eden after he had transgressed God's Law and partook of the forbidden fruit.

God essentially asked, "Adam, where are you at?" and Adam replied, "God, the woman You gave to me-she gave me the fruit and I ate."

Adam tried to shift the blame, saying, "Yes, God, I ate the fruit because You gave me the woman, and she gave me the fruit. If You hadn't given me that woman, she couldn't have given me the fruit. And if she hadn't give me the fruit, I wouldn't have eaten it. Then, You and I would still be cool."

THE BLAME GAME

Thousands of years later, man continues to play the same "blame game" Adam invented.

Rev. Craft blamed the Lord.

"God, I'm still a junkie," he'd say, "because You created the poppy seeds that other people transform into heroin powder. When it was brought into my neighborhood, You permitted me to get a taste of it one time through my cousin, The Weasel. I liked the high, but You could've stopped me at any point. You could've fixed it so I never came into contact with that stuff. Or, You could have struck Jimmy down with lightning from heaven. But You permitted me to get high. So, God, I know that You permitted me to sample heroin."

"Now I've become addicted," he'd continue, "and I'm enslaved to it. God, I'm trusting You now to bring me out of drugs since it must have been Your will that I'm a junkie. Otherwise, I would have never gotten hooked in the first place."

Does any of that sound familiar to you?

It ought to, since "the blame game" started with Adam. Through the centuries, man has become much better at playing it. Rev. Craft took "the blame game" to the next level when he had the audacity to blame God for his addiction to drugs.

SIN'S DECEITFUL NATURE

Rev. Craft's reasoning was foolish, but sinners are never logical. That is why the Bible talks about the deceitfulness of sin. It has a way of making us believe lies and disbelieve the truth.

But exhort one another daily, while it is called

today; lest any of you be hardened through the deceitfulness of sin.

(Hebrews 3:13, KJV)

Godly grief arises from the ownership of sin.

For change to occur, Rev. Craft could no longer blame God for being a junkie. He had to own up to his sin and say...

"Yes, God, I did that."

"God, I went out with my first cousin, Jimmy, and got on that train where we rode up to the South Bronx to 175th Street and Bathgate Avenue. I rode the 3rd Avenue El and the 7th Avenue express down to 116th Street and Lenox Avenue where I got off the train with him. I walked with him around the corner and bought that dope. I sat with him as he went into the next apartment and entered the shooting gallery. I was with him when he paid the two dollars for us to get a set of works. I sat with him and watched him put the heroin in the bottle cap, put water in the dropper, and cook it up with matches. I put the piece of belt around my left arm and watched my vein pop up. I watched him draw my shot of dope into the dropper and hook the needle on the end. I stuck that needle in my arm and watched the blood go up as I injected that heroin in my arm. Lord, I did that."

Do you see it?

Rev. Craft needed to take ownership.

Instead, he permitted the deceitfulness of sin and Satan to open him up to a spirit the Bible calls "witch-craft" or "sorcery." Satan had access, through the spirit of witchcraft, to take control of his body, soul and spirit because of habitual sin, then saying, "Lord, I am sorry."

Rev. Craft would then go to church the following Sunday and kneel at the altar, saying, "Lord, forgive me."

The deception made matters worse.

Rev. Craft deceived himself into believing that God's forgiveness and mercy were going to protect him from a physical or an eternal death.

In reality, He was protected, but that protection had nothing to do with what Rev. Craft believed. The only reason he did not die was because God's grace and mercy were in full force.

THE DEATH HERITAGE

So many around Steven held death sentences.

Jimmy and Hershel (his cousins), his own natural brother, Gary, and Rev. Craft were all drug addicts. Hershel died from an overdose of cocaine; Gary died from AIDS contracted by main lining; Jimmy is dead from an overdose on heroin.

The only reason Rev. Craft is not dead is because God's grace and mercy rose up in him and fostered a godly grief and sorrow that made him take ownership of his sin and not shift the blame.

The words that changed his life were, "Lord, I'm wrong. Help me."

When you begin to declare "Lord, I'm wrong" in your own heart, God can then begin to set the stage for your deliverance.

ROCKY SURRENDERS

Rocky's life experiences were different from Rev. Craft's, but they both ultimately needed to experience the godly sorrow that brings repentance.

Rocky had been seeking the things of the world, trying many different devices in an attempt to experience some type of peace. But one day in 1993, in an office in the Northern Bronx, Rocky had a conversation with an ex-partner and friend of his on the force named Samuel Robinson.

Samuel was fond of asking him, "Rocky, what are you really looking for in life?"

As Rocky shared some of his past experiences, and explained his quest for peace, Samuel pointed out to him that it was not enough to have certain qualities in life, but that he had to surrender to the Lordship of Jesus Christ.

When Samuel shared his own personal reality with Jesus, Rocky began to understand that all of the things he had done in his own strength, whether they were good or bad, would not be enough to get him to heaven, or to give him peace on earth.

Rocky's concept of heaven was that he would get there through addition and subtraction. If he did ten good things and only five bad things, then he had "a plus five" credits to get him into heaven. It was Samuel who pointed out to Rocky that you cannot earn your way into heaven.

He told Rocky that the formula was simple: he only needed to confess his sins, and surrender his life to Jesus Christ as his Lord and Savior.

The first time Rocky heard "the formula," he did not respond. However, on the second evening when Rocky heard that simple solution to life's peace, he went home and surrendered his life to Christ after being lovingly confronted by Samuel Robinson.

"Did you make your commitment to give your life to Christ yet?," Samuel asked him.

"No, I haven't. Not yet," Rocky replied. "I know I have no excuse."

So, after leaving work, Rocky went home, got down on his knees, and said a simple prayer.

"Lord Jesus," he prayed, "I ask You to be my Lord

and Savior. Please come into my life and forgive me of all my sins."

In that moment when Rocky was all alone, he realized that he had finally owned up to his sins, and that this was the only way to real happiness. When he confessed true repentance, a spiritual light of understanding went off in his mind and heart.

He knew he'd never be the same.

His transformation, although it might not have been a spiritual explosion, occurred when he took ownership of all the sins he had committed...of all the wrong relationships, of all the evil thoughts, of virtually everything wrong and sinful in his life.

When Rocky gave all of that up and acknowledged Jesus as Lord and Savior, he began to truly understand repentance for the first time.

CRAFT'S FUTILE MOVE TO THE WEST COAST

Rev. Craft needed to come to the same conclusions about repentance as Rocky.

Steven saw all of his cousins, all of his running buddies in his family, die from drug-related situations. Yet, Satan convinced him in his own fog of criminal-thinking that circumstances, people, and situations (external factors) were his problem and the cause of his struggles with drugs.

Steven honestly but incorrectly believed that a change of environment would fix the problem.

So, in order to not have his cousins around to tempt him, he decided to move from New York to Los Angeles. When he arrived in Los Angeles, he was clean (free from drugs) for about three days.

The Bible says that as soon as "the cares of this world," or the problems of life, begin to take hold of our spirit, emptiness is the result, the void God created in every one of us that only He can fill. In Los Angeles, Steven once again felt that grating emptiness, that hollow feeling like a dead, dry log rotting from the inside. As he experienced the emptiness and drugs once again, he began to realize that his problem was not with his cousins, or with his New York neighborhood, but his problem was on the inside.

The problem was spiritual!

Steven's drug problem had nothing to do with New York City or Los Angeles or Jimmy, Hershel, or Gary...it had to do with Steven's heart! People would call him a "church hypocrite," and he would boldly tell them, "You have no right to judge me! God knows my heart, and God knows that a man's heart is 'wicked and utterly deceitful.'"

Since those words are in the Bible, Steven was speaking true words about man's heart. Who can know man's heart but God? However, Steven was trying to twist the truth to make it seem like God was in agreement with his mess. In fact, God knew that Steven's heart was wicked, deceitful and evil, and He knew the FULL extent of that corruption.

Even though he was in new surroundings, Steven began "chasing the bag" once again. The heroin on the West Coast was Mexican brown heroin, and it was stronger; it was uncut compared to the heroin on the East Coast; it did not have the cuts of China White heroin. As Steven began to use Mexican heroin, he came under addiction and bondage to the enemy even faster because it took a smaller dose of brown Mexican powder to cause addiction.

As a result of the Los Angeles experience, Satan brought Steven into an even greater bondage by introducing him to a new drug he had never experienced in New York called Angel Dust or PCP. At the time he did not realize that it was a lethal combination – smoking PCP along with the heroin addiction.

Then, he began to drink.

STRAIGHT JACKET AND GETTING STRAIGHT

One day, Steven found himself totally in a frame of psychosis on Venice Beach, right outside of Los Angeles on the Pacific Ocean. He woke up in a straight jacket in Camarillo State Hospital for mental patients, far removed from Los Angeles.

To this day, Rev. Craft has no real recollection of

that horrendous event in the mid '70's. He cannot recall any of the circumstances involved in what happened; he does not know how he ended up at the hospital; he can only assume that an ambulance or police car took him there.

When he regained consciousness, he was like the Prodigal Son who finally came to realize the depravation of his life when in a pigpen. Steven "came to himself" buck-naked in a straight jacket in a mental ward.

For the first time, he saw his life in reality and truth.

For the first time, he took full ownership of his multitude of sins.

For the first time, he experienced godly sorrow in his total helplessness. He was totally vulnerable, naked for security reasons, and helpless (the straight jacket kept him immobile). In a room with no windows (except for the observation window for the guards to watch him), and knowing that he was in a mental hospital, he saw reality and realized it was called "sin" and "rebellion." For once in his life, he was really afraid. He had no way of knowing, at that particular time, if he ever was going to recover.

Steven knew he had not literally lost his mind, but he was committed in a mental ward, and he was not sure how he arrived there.

"It was like waking up in a horror movie. I tried to communicate to the psychiatrist on duty as he made his rounds, telling him that I only remembered blacking out on Venice Beach. Of course, I didn't tell him I was using multiple drugs and drinking, though they already knew I had a drug episode."

Steven tried to convince the psychiatrist that he was now fine, and asked to be discharged.

"You're not going anywhere," the doctor replied.

So, Steven remained in that mental hospital where the drugs began to wear off. Like the prodigal son who came to himself in a pigsty, Steven asked, "What am I doing here?" He realized it was time to stop his sinful life and give his life over completely to God.

"As I sat in that room, with no clothes on, totally vulnerable, restrained in a straight jacket, in a locked unit where other people had serious mental conditions, all my hope was gone. God knew that He now had my full, undivided attention. There was nothing left in me to buck against Him. I knew that the only help I was going to get had to come from heaven."

Steven took ownership of his sins.

He began to seek God in prayer from the depths of his heart. He prayed, "Lord, if You get me out of this place and help me, if You'll deliver me out of this mess, I will serve You the rest of my life."

Something inside of him broke.

All the games, all the habitual sinning, all "the sorry games," then going back and doing the same thing, seemed blown away in a puff of smoke. For the first time in his life, Steven saw clearly just how wretched, wicked, sinful, and evil he was.

A CHANGED HEART

Godly sorrow gripped his heart and opened up the door to bring the fruit of repentance which was a changed heart.

Before, he was playing "the sorry game" and telling others:

"Don't judge me. God knows my heart. When He is ready to clean me up, God will do it. I don't need you, or anybody else, to tell me how to live. God knows my struggles, my weaknesses. God knows my spirit is willing but my flesh is weak. When God's ready for me to live holy, God will fix it. So, get out of my face and leave me alone."

Yes, God knew Steven's heart was deceitful and utterly wicked; God knew the depths of it; yet, He permitted the circumstances to happen on Venice Beach to bring an end to the deception.

Stevie Louis Craft was the enemy of Stevie Louis Craft.

Unless God intervened and pulled the plug on his games, Stevie Louis Craft would have died in his sins and perished in Hell. But God brought him to a place where He could get Stevie's undivided attention in the mental institution. As a result, God opened up the door through grief.

Steven had real grief.

He no longer said, "I'm sorry I got busted" and it ended there. Now he prayed, "Lord, I am afraid. I'm scared. These people want to commit me. I can't call anybody to get me out of here because my family is 3,000 miles East. Even if they were here they couldn't get me out. God, the only hope I have now is You."

Steven called on the invisible God who he claimed knew his heart. God responded because He knew that Steven was now ready; he no longer had a phony, hypocritical religiosity. His sorrow was real, pure and godly, one that leads to the fruit of repentance which, in turn, leads to salvation and deliverance.

Steven was suddenly aware of his obligation to his Lord and Savior, Jesus Christ. For once in his life he saw the Gospel, not "religiosity." He finally under-

stood that Jesus Christ came as a Perfect Man who was God in the flesh, and lived a perfect life without sin for 33 years. He was our Role Model who made an unequal and uneven exchange.

Him who knew no sin he made to be sin on our

*behalf; that we might become the righteousness
of God in him.*

(2 Corinthians 5:21, ASV)

Steven began to understand that Jesus took his
sin in an unequal exchange and gave him His righteousness. He took his wickedness and gave His holiness.

Steven was finally ready to receive God's free gift.

THE UNMERITED GIFT

We all want to receive a gift when we think we can
come out on the better side of the deal. Steven finally understood the Good News that Jesus Christ came
to earth, perfect, to die and to take on his sin of heroin addiction. Steven began to see that when he put
the needle in his arm, he was putting the needle in
Christ's arm. When he was cussing, swearing, and
being a religious hypocrite and a junky, he was putting it on Him.

Jesus willingly takes on the sins of every human
being ever created on the planet...because He loves us
so. God said:

> *[16]For God so loved the world, that he gave his
> only begotten Son, that whosoever believeth in
> him should not perish, but have everlasting
> life.*

> *[17]For God sent not his Son into the world to
> condemn the world; but that the world
> through him might be saved.*

[18]He that believeth on him is not condemned: but he that believeth not is condemned already, because he hath not believed in the name of the only begotten Son of God.

[19]And this is the condemnation, that light is come into the world, and men loved darkness rather than light, because their deeds were evil.

[20]For every one that doeth evil hateth the light, neither cometh to the light, lest his deeds should be reproved.

(John 3:16-20, KJV)

Steven loved the darkness of the shooting galleries, the darkness of the West Side of Harlem, the darkness of the bar scene in the Bronx, the darkness of New Jersey. He loved that darkness more than he loved the light of holiness.

His deeds were evil, and he knew it.

That is why he would shoot dope behind closed doors in a shooting gallery with somebody looking through the peephole just in case the narcs knocked down the door.

When Steven needed a fix, he always hid, either in a stairwell, or on a roof, or in somebody's house.

It wasn't until God stripped away that darkness and produced Godly grief in his life that he could change and see the bondages of sin in his life.

He could almost hear God saying:

"This is what you have permitted the devil to bring upon you. He has stripped you naked. He has stripped your dignity and he'll take your life. He has brought you into slavery and bondage. Now he wants to take your mind so you cannot comprehend the glorious Gospel of Jesus Christ. He wants to take your soul into an everlasting hell.

"Are you ready to own up to your sin?"

Godly sorrow opened the door to repentance.

AN OBLIGATION TO HIM

Rocky found his obligation to His Savior was overwhelming.

He also had to reach the point where he owned up to his sinful lifestyle. But, as he began to grow and understand the things of the Lord, he began to comprehend that he was purchased and bought with a price. Jesus Christ had, in fact, taken all of his sins upon Himself when He went to the cross of Calvary.

Rocky became aware, at the time of his conversion, that he no longer belonged to himself; from that point on, anything he would do in life was out of an obligation to Christ.

He began to reflect on some of his exploits and past experiences and started to realize that his life was no longer his own...that it was purchased with a price. Rocky began to understand that he was created to serve Christ.

Ultimately, he became acutely aware of his obligation. The things that he had once done were no longer desires for him. Fornication ended, and it was paramount in his mind that he conduct himself in a Godly manner with his counterparts and peers at work.

Even the way he dealt with the people out on the street changed. Whether they were the perpetrators or the victims of a crime, Rocky started to look at them, and treat them, in a Christ-like manner.

Rocky no longer cared what others thought, or what the world taught. He simply decided to walk in obedience to what God wanted him to do.

That is where the obligation came in.

God gave him another opportunity, and his gratitude was expressed by doing the things God had called him to do. From the day of Rocky's repentance, he held that obligation up as a banner as He served the risen Christ who is his Lord and Savior. Until the day God calls him home, he will still be obligated to Him.

When you were a child growing up, your parents seemed to instinctively have a way of making you feel obligated to them. This obligation was based on the fact that they had given you birth. It was not an obligation to do the things they wanted you to do because you loved them...it was an obligation because they had given you birth! That was enough for them to dictate to you without having to give you "just cause" as to why you had to do the things they called you to do.

But with the Lord it is different.

There was an obligation because Rocky knew all that the Lord Jesus Christ had done: He had purchased us with a price. And, it was but a small thing for us to do the things that He had called upon us to do. For Rocky, his obligation weighed heavily in his heart and in his vocation as a police officer.

THE TWO OBLIGATIONS

On July 28, 1983, at the New York City Police Academy, Rocky took the oath to become a police officer and to uphold the constitution of our great nation. He took that oath earnestly and soberly, with strong conviction. By far, he considered that oath to be one of the most important decisions he had made up to that point (he was 21 years of age).

But, it was not until the Lord began to draw him to the final place where he surrendered his life to Him that he felt all the other important decisions in his life were overshadowed.

Rocky was obligated to the inhabitants of New York City because they paid him a good salary and gave him a solid career. His profession gave him a sense of satisfaction as an individual; he was performing an occupation that was unique, and that blessed him with financial security.

But, the obligation Rocky felt for his Savior on that day gave him life! Not the old life he once knew, but the life that he now lives, and the eternal life that is to come. Because of the most important decision of his entire life, he now knows that he will forever reign with Jesus Christ in heaven.

Nothing on this earth will ever be remotely near what our Lord and Savior has in store for us.

The obligation parents tend to impress upon their children is not the kind of obligation Rocky has for his Savior today. The obligation he has to Him is because He saved his soul, body, and spirit.

"ALL SOULS ARE MINE"

As a former drug addict, Steven Craft is still astounded and amazed as he thinks about how God had miraculously delivered him *literally* from death. As we shared earlier, death was all around Rev. Craft. He saw two of his first cousins and his baby brother all die from the devastation of drugs.

Yet, even though Steven was doing the same things they were doing, he was still alive! Now, like Rocky, he too had an obligation to give back to others by being a living witness. This testimony book is written by both of us so it will serve as a small seed, an offering to God, to let people know that everything we have in our lives today now belongs to Him!

Behold, all souls are mine; as the soul of the father, so also the soul of the son is mine: the soul that sinneth, it shall die.
(Ezekiel 18:4 KJV)
(emphasis added by authors)

He created us! The Bible says we are not our own. We are bought with a price. We did not create ourselves—God created us. Therefore, we are obligated to Him once for our creation and twice because of our redemption.

It is a dual obligation.

Every human being is obligated to God because God is our Maker. No one can say, "I don't need God. If He'll leave me alone, I'll leave Him alone."

How do you think you arrived on this planet?

Evolution?

If you exist, you did not evolve, no matter what lies you have been told about your origins. You were created by the Creator, and you owe your Creator because He gave you life, your physical existence.

We all are born into sin, but if you are spiritually born again, God has also given you eternal life. We are all born into sin and iniquity-born to die and go to hell. But with God, with His mercy and grace, He reached down to us and brought us into a place of Godly sorrow, which produces repentance which leads to salvation.

PRAY OUT LOUD TO HIM!

As Godly grief (pure grief) arises in our hearts, we take ownership of our sins and become acutely sensitive to our obligation to the One who created us, saved us, died for us, and rose for us, and wants to give us an eternal hope in heaven with Him forever.

True grief causes us to ache with an overwhelming sorrow for our sins. Once Godly sorrow begins to work deep repentance in our hearts, it leads to overwhelming sorrow (not the "I'm sorry I got caught" game).

If you are experiencing true sorrow as you read this book, or even if you need to re-dedicate yourself to God, would you say this simple prayer out loud?

"I'm sorry, Lord, that I have sinned against You, that I have taken this life You gave me, this body You gave me, this mind that You gave me, these gifts, abilities, talents, and resources You gave me...and squandered them on my own lusts.

"Lord, I'm sorry because I have sinned against You and done evil in Your sight. I'm sorry because I have offended You...my Creator, my Redeemer, my Savior, my Deliverer, my Soon-coming King. From this day forward I am obligated until my eyes close in death. I will do with my life whatever You want me to do with it because my life is not my life anymore. It is Your life! You gave it to me.

"Like Job said, 'The Lord giveth and the Lord has the power to taketh away. Blessed be the name of the Lord.'"

"Thank You, Father, for the gift of life, and for the gift of salvation. Amen."

If you said this prayer with sincerity, then your Godly grief and pain will produce a repentance that leads and contributes to salvation and deliverance from evil, and it never brings regret.

Before giving your life to Christ, many report to us that they feel much like a dog constantly chasing its tail, not knowing why the tail was created, or what was its purpose.

After salvation, all lives change, and the tail-chasing days cease.

In the world's eyes, Rocky was a respected police officer earning a good salary, but he did not know his Savior during most of that time. It wasn't until he began to feel true grief and sorrow for the things he had done to his Lord and Savior, Jesus Christ, that his life started to change.

Before his conversion, his behavior, speech, and thoughts did not line up with God's desire for his life. After his conversion, he did not want to do anything to feel that kind of grief and ache again.

Real sorrow comes from doing things in contradiction to God's rules for our lives. Real sorrow is more than just a hypocritical showing of some superficial semblance of remorse.

It is more than a confession without conviction.

Real, overwhelming sorrow is always accompanied by grief and an entrenched determination not to sin again. Only God can give you the feeling, the determination, by way of the Holy Spirit, to do the things that He has called you to do.

When Godly grief and sorrow get hold of your heart, it activates you, in obedience, to surrender to the Lordship of Christ Jesus.

CRY OUT TO GOD

In Rev. Craft's life, as he cried out to God in that mental hospital, totally wretched and undone, when he cried out to God from his inner-most being, he instinctively knew that God had heard his prayer.

There was no audible voice.

Nobody supernaturally appeared in his room; no bright light beamed down on his face. But he instinctively knew that God had heard his cry, and that something had changed on the inside.

Peace came over him, enveloping him, even though he was still without clothes, wrapped in a restraining jacket. Steven sat in that room with a supernatural knowing that everything was going to be all right, even though he had no idea how this thing was going to work.

Something was different.

It took four days before the doctors released him from the hospital. But Steven knew his heart had changed, and that heart-transformation was causing his thinking to change.

His lifestyle changed from that time forward; he never returned to that old, destructive life.

CHAPTER NINE

New Lives, New Experiences, New Hope

When Steven left the mental hospital and climbed on that bus, heading back to Los Angeles, he knew this was a new and different time in his life.

His peaceful feelings did not match his reality.

He had no money in his pocket and no where to live. His financial resources were exhausted. Yet, he somehow knew in his heart that if he could only get to a church, it would help him stay close to God.

"I've got to get to church," Steven thought. He knew now that the bar wasn't his answer, and that drugs were not his answer. This time he determined to find his answer in a church.

TAKE THE CRUMBS!

God led Steven to The Crenshaw Christian Center, Pastor Fred Price's church on Crenshaw Boulevard in Inglewood (a suburb of Los Angeles). He spoke with the Rev. Fred Price and explained his situation to him in a form of honesty he had not used before in his life.

"I was honest with him and told him everything. I told him that I had just come down from Camarillo State Hospital where I had spent four days for a drug psychosis. I told him I was a former heroin addict, and that I was trying to get my life together. I told him I was homeless and jobless. I told him everything that would have given him complete cause to totally reject me."

Steven was determined to change.

Remember the story in the Bible about the woman with the demon-possessed daughter? She came to Jesus and essentially said, "My daughter is grievously vexed with the devil and I'm not even a Jew. I'm a Canaanite. But I know You can heal her."

Jesus looked at her and said, "Woman, it is not appropriate for Me to give the children's bread to dogs."

Now, upon hearing that, the mother could have become offended and left. Had she done so, she would have missed her blessing.

Instead, she saw something deeper. She saw the miracles Jesus had performed for others, so she replied, "True Lord, even the dogs eat the crumbs that fall from the Master's table."

Jesus marveled at her answer and her faith.

"Woman, go to your house," He told her. "Your daughter is whole."

That story is so powerful!

God's crumbs were far better than anything the world ever had to offer!

When Steven stood in Fred Price's office with nothing but the clothes on his back, pitiful, wretched and undone, he was changed and humbled...and willing to accept any crumb the church could offer.

All of "the game" had gone out of him. All the habitual sinning, sorrying, and hardness of heart, all the slavery was gone. Steven cried out to God because he had finally taken ownership of his sins; he now had an obligation to the One who saved him from death and released him from the bondage of drugs and the literal bondage of insanity.

Steven declared, "Man of God, I believe God sent me to you for you to help me, and I'm not leaving this church until you do."

When Steven, in obedient surrender, purposed in his heart not to be deterred, God permitted him to be tested through Rev. Fred Price. The man of God started pacing back and forth in his office, and finally said, "You realize that this church is not a bank."

"I know it's not a bank, sir," Steven replied, "but I

know you're a minister of the Gospel and I need help. I've laid it all out on the line for you. I have hidden nothing. And furthermore, I'm not leaving your presence until you help me."

Rev. Price began to pace up and down again. Then he replied, "What do you want?"

"I need a job, a place to stay, and some food to eat."

Rev. Price then took Steven down to the local cab company where he paid $50 for Steven to take the taxi examination. As a result, he was given a taxi permit to drive a cab which paid in cash money at the end of every day.

That met the immediate need for a job.

Then, Rev. Price took him to the welfare office where Steven obtained a voucher for a little hole-in-the-wall, roach-infested hotel room in Los Angeles. That met the need for shelter.

Rev. Price then obtained food vouchers for Steven so he could eat in the greasy spoon café underneath the hotel. That took care of his food.

Finally, Rev. Price obtained a clothing voucher so Steven could go to the Salvation Army and pick some clothes off of a rack. That took care of his clothing.

His needs (not his wants) were met.

Of course, Steven was not excited about staying in a roach-infested hotel with a common bath down the hall. He didn't want to eat in that greasy spoon. He didn't want to go to the Salvation Army to pick out used clothes.

But just like the mother who persisted with God until her daughter was delivered, Steven persisted with the man of God, and his needs were met.

THE PROCESS OF TRANSFORMATION

For the next six months, Steven drove that Yellow Cab, receiving a bit of cash at the end of each shift.

For the next six months, he'd go back to his hotel room, wash up, go downstairs to the restaurant, use his food voucher to get a hot meal, then he'd take the bus over to the church.

Every day.

For six months.

No matter what the activity was, Steven went, even though that church activity might have nothing to do with him. He'd sit in the corner of the church and quietly absorb whatever was being taught. He knew that to go back to drugs meant his destruction, so he followed this same process of transformation for six months straight, without fail.

And God honored his faithfulness!

As a result of being around Christian people, of being in a place where he was hearing the Word of

God three to four times a week, in Bible studies and in worship services, he began to grow because of his obedience to surrender. He surrendered his desires and the lusts of his flesh to Christ.

When he became tempted to go down to the corner and see what the fellows were doing, he resisted the temptation, knowing that it would only end in death.

SUBMIT, RESIST, AND DEFEAT TEMPTATION

Submit yourselves therefore to God. Resist the devil, and he will flee from you.
(James 4:7, KJV)

Young people in the world today are told to fight temptation by yielding to it. If you yield to temptation, you are not fighting it.

It slays you.

The only way to fight temptation is to run from it or resist it.

How can you fight temptation by giving in to it? Once you give in to it, the fight is over. You lose. So, our young people are being deceived by misguided adults.

There is a movie that fits today's society called "Fight the Temptation." It espouses a philosophy that says, "Don't fight the feeling. Just do it." That is a lie from hell! Satan's message is, "If you're tempted, do it." Satan knows he can only tempt us to do evil, and the moment we step into the realm of doing it, he reels us in. We're entrapped.

One of the reasons we wrote *Virtue and Vice* is so people will know that the *only way* to fight temptation is to resist it, to run from it, to stand against it, to oppose it.

That message is not being taught, but it is a message of truth, a message of common sense.

As we have shared before, godly grief produces godly sorrow which brings about true repentance and a changed heart which then lead to a changed mind and a changed lifestyle.

THE PROCESS PRODUCES FRUIT

Steven honored God during his six months of doing that which was right, faithfully and consistently, day in and day out.

Ultimately, God gave him a wife, Edith Mae Austin who he met in the church. She had two daughters, Monette and Yvette, from a previous, failed first marriage.

Edith Mae and Steven were married in 1978, and Steven had to now learn how to be a husband and a father. From a lifestyle of being totally selfish and self-centered, he was transformed and challenged to learn how to become a Godly father in a ready-made family. He had to learn how to cope with all of the problems involved with being a step-parent, while his new wife and daughters were learning how to cope with the pain they had suffered from the wrong choices of the wife's first husband and the daughters' real father.

God strengthened Steven and taught him how to take on the new responsibilities, not just for his own life, but also for the lives of two, innocent young girls (8 and 12 years old at the time of the marriage). Because their father chose to go into an adulterous relationship, and because his Godly wife wanted to serve the Lord as a family unit, he decided to abandon his family and go off with another woman to satisfy his own lust.

God sent Steven to become those girls' stepfather. It was difficult for him because he did not know how to take care of himself, let alone be a father. So, in one "fell-swoop" he had to learn how to be a father and a husband. Each time there was a conflict, his new wife was caught in the middle because she was his newlywed wife, and still a mother who wanted to protect her two girls.

They all had to grow and were stretched through that process. It took many years before the girls actually understood that Steven was there for them, committed to their mother, and to the girls, for the long haul.

Steven learned that as He obeys God and surrenders to His will, God takes us into levels of growth and maturity where we have never been.

You cannot imagine how far God will take you when you are obedient and surrender totally to Him.

CHAPTER TEN

Ten Spiritual Basics
to Revolutionize Your Life

Godly grief brings Godly sorrow, which brings repentance, which is the result of God's moral law that is written in our hearts, better known as the Ten Commandments. These Ten Commandments, as recorded in Exodus 20 (KJV), are as follows:

THE FIRST COMMANDMENT

¹And God spake all these words, saying

²I am the Lord thy God, which have brought thee out of the land of Egypt, out of the house of bondage.

³Thou shalt have no other gods before me.

THE SECOND COMMANDMENT

⁴Thou shalt not make unto thee any graven image, or any likeness of any thing that is in heaven above, or that is in the earth beneath, or that is in the water under the earth.

⁵Thou shalt not bow down thyself to them, nor serve them: for I the LORD thy God am a jealous God, visiting the iniquity of the fathers upon the children unto the third and fourth generation of them that hate me;

⁶And shewing mercy unto thousands of them that love me, and keep my commandments.

THIRD COMMANDMENT

⁷Thou shalt not take the name of the LORD thy God in vain; for the LORD will not hold him guiltless that taketh his name in vain.

THE FOURTH COMMANDMENT

⁸Remember the Sabbath day, to keep it holy.

⁹Six days shalt thou labour, and do all thy work:

¹⁰But the seventh day is the Sabbath of the LORD thy God: in it thou shalt not do any work, thou, nor thy son, nor thy daughter, thy manservant, nor thy maidservant, nor thy cattle, nor thy stranger that is within thy gates:

¹¹For in six days the LORD made heaven and earth, the sea, and all that in them is, and rested the seventh day: wherefore the LORD blessed the Sabbath day, and hallowed it.

THE FIFTH COMMANDMENT

¹²Honour thy father and thy mother: that thy days may be long upon the land which the LORD thy God giveth thee.

THE SIXTH COMMANDMENT

¹³Thou shalt not kill.

THE SEVENTH COMMANDMENT

¹⁴Thou shalt not commit adultery.

THE EIGHTH COMMANDMENT

¹⁵Thou shalt not steal.

THE NINTH COMMANDMENT

¹⁶Thou shalt not bear false witness against thy neighbour.

THE TENTH COMMANDMENT

¹⁷Thou shalt not covet thy neighbour's house, thou shalt not covet thy neighbour's wife, nor his manservant, nor his maidservant, nor his ox, nor his ass, nor any thing that is thy neighbour's."

These Ten Commandments are God's moral law, and provide the ten spiritual basics to revolutionize your life.

WRITE THESE LAWS ON YOUR HEART

When Rev. Craft and Rocky were non-believers, they took all of these laws for granted.

In Rocky's case, his job and his sinful relationship became his personal idols (against the First Commandment). Before he came to know Christ, these Commandments had absolutely no meaning to him. He lived his life according to his feelings and thoughts, doing what was best for Rocky.

But when he was transformed, God's Law was written upon his heart!

Rocky began to understand that the Ten Commandments are not a bunch of stupid rules God arbitrarily gave to man; instead, he recognized that they were the platform and format by which God intended man to live life in the fullest of possible joy.

It grieves us that in this modern day the Ten Commandments are taken for granted, ignored, and even outlawed in public places. Our courts are doing their best to try and take the Ten Commandments out of our laws and out of our way of life.

What a sad contradiction that is from a historical standpoint. Our wise forefathers drafted our new country's rules and laws, statutes, and governments based upon God's Ten Commandments. Yet now, this same country is trying to exclude God and eradicate Him from every aspect of our culture and society.

What a sad commentary!

We pray that our nation will wake up and cry out, "Lord, we do not know what we are doing at this particular time. Please cause Your laws to be written on man's heart once again to bring conviction, conversion, and redemption. Otherwise, our country is doomed to live an ungodly, deadly lifestyle."

To experience real grief from sin, it must be activated as the result of knowing that God's moral law is written in the heart of every human being— white, black, young, old, rich, poor – from every culture.

NONE GOOD ENOUGH!

Reverend Ray Comfort, an evangelist God uses mightily, wrote a tract entitled "Are You Good Enough To Go To Heaven?" In that tract he explains how the Law of God is placed in the heart of every human being to lead us to repentance.

Romans 3:23 says :

For all have sinned, and come short of the glory of God.

All human beings have sinned and come short of the glory of God, and there are none righteous in themselves, no not one. The glory of God is the standard God sets.

When Rocky compared himself to his fellow squad detectives, he would think, "Yes, I do lust after women in my mind, but at least I'm not as bad as that old sex offender over there."

At the time, Rocky did not understand that there are none righteous, no not one. God did not see him through his own silly standard ("I'm not as bad as that guy"), but through His own Holy Standard.

Many on the police force somehow felt that they were invincible and not subject to laws because they were policemen. Fortunately, Rocky understood that when a policeman did an immoral or illegal action, even with the cop's badge to try and hide behind, there was always the possibility that the law-breaker could go to prison.

Reverend Ray Comfort, in his Gospel tract, asks all of the questions you will ask yourself in life, including, "Am I good enough to go to heaven?"

The answer to that question is another question.

"Have you obeyed the Ten Commandments?"

Most would answer, "Well, I've broken one or two, but nothing too serious like murder or rape."

Perhaps as we take a few pages here to review these Commandments from a more personal perspective, you may change your concept of "nothing too serious" to "Yes, I have failed to obey God's Law."

CHAPTER ELEVEN

The Regular Guy's Ten Commandments

Let us take a few moments here for you, to review these Ten Commandments in more basic language to help you understand God's intent, and to help you better see how your walk is with God.

THE FIRST COMMANDMENT:

I am the LORD thy God, which brought thee out of the land of Egypt, from the house of bondage.

(Deuteronomy 5:6, KJV)

Ask yourself these questions:

"Is God first in my life?"

"Do I love God above all else?"

There are many types of false gods. Your false god could be anything that controls or dominates your life, such as a hobby, an addiction, or even a television set.

If we love anything...husband, wife, children or even our own lives, more than we love God, we are setting our affections on the gift rather than the Giver (a transgression of the First Commandment). In fact, the Bible says that we should so love God that our affection for mother, father, brother, sister, wife, or husband would pale in comparison. After all, it is God who gave those other loved ones to us in the first place.

Jesus also commanded us to love our neighbors as much as we love ourselves. He spoke of the Samaritan who found an injured stranger and bathed his wounds, then carried him to the inn where he gave the inn owner money for his care. Today, that man is called the "good Samaritan," but in reality he wasn't good at all. He merely obeyed the basic commandment to love his neighbor as much as he loved himself. God expects us to love our fellow human beings as much as we love ourselves, whether they are friends or enemies.

Have you loved God with all your heart?

Have you loved humanity as much as you love yourself?

You be your own judge; we are not judging you, only asking you to ask the questions.

Finally, you should understand that the sentence for breaking the First Commandment is death.

THE SECOND COMMANDMENT:

Thou shalt not make thee any graven image, or any likeness of any thing that is in heaven above, or that is in the earth beneath, or that is in the waters beneath the earth.

(Deuteronomy 5:6, KJV)

Do not try and create a false god to serve you, either with your hands or with your mind.

For example, Rocky's god did not mind "a little white lie" here and there. In fact, Rocky's god had no moral dictates at all. Of course, in truth, his god did not exist, but was merely a figment of his own imagination, an image shaped in his mind to suit himself and his sinful lifestyle.

For some, their god is money. For others, their version of god is some kind of a crutch, a genie in a bottle that they turn to when their backs are against the wall. If you have any other god, then you received a death sentence.

Is your god the One revealed in the Holy Bible?

If not, then you have made your own god to suit yourself. You have committed the oldest sin in the Bible. Scripture warns that no idolater will enter the Kingdom of Heaven.

Steven had conjured up his version of a god in his own mind, a god who would not judge him for his sins, because his god could only judge him when he was ready to take away Steven's addiction to drugs.

Steven's god did not really exist.

The God of the Bible says,

I tell you, Nay: but, except ye repent, ye shall all likewise perish.
(Luke 13:3, KJV)

Follow peace with all men, and holiness, without which no man shall see the Lord.
(Hebrews 12:14, KJV)

Steven made an idol of a false god to suit his sin, giving him two death sentences.

The sentence for breaking the Second Commandment is still death.

THE THIRD COMMANDMENT

Thou shalt not take the name of the LORD thy God in vain: for the LORD will not hold him guiltless that taketh his name in vain.
(Deuteronomy 5:11, KJV)

Have you ever taken God's Name in vain?

To express your disgust, have you used His Holy Name in anger?

Imagine...even Hitler's name was not despised enough to be used as a curse word. If you use God's Holy Name in a cursing manner, you are a blasphemer and you will not enter the Kingdom of God.

A less obvious way to take God's Name in vain is

to openly call yourself a "Christian" but live like a heathen. Your sinful lifestyle, combined with your declaration that "I am a Christian" bears a bad witness to others, and slurs the Holy Name of Jesus Christ. Gandhi was said to say something like this after observing how the British Christians so freely perpetrated murder and other evils upon the Indian people: "Were it not for the lives of the Christians I see around me, I might have been inclined to investigate the Christian religion in a closer manner."

The sentence for taking the Name of the LORD in vain, for breaking this Commandment, is death.

THE FOURTH COMMANDMENT

Keep the sabbath day to sanctify it, as the LORD thy God hath commanded thee.
(Deuteronomy 5:12, KJV)

Rocky ignored this Commandment for 22 years, even though God gave him the gift of life. Never once did he ask God what He required of him. He was guilty of breaking this Commandment.

When Steven was shooting dope, he did not care anything about the Lord's day. The furthest thing from his mind was getting up and going to church. He got there when he got there. He did everything on the Sabbath day but keep it holy.

In America today, there is every possible distraction to draw Christians away from Sunday service.

There are baseball games, football games, soccer games, hockey games, plays, musical theater, hobbies, and so on.

"Sunday is my time to rest" seems to be the anthem of many Christians and non-Christians alike. "I work too hard to be going to church on Sunday. God knows I love Him, and that's all that matters."

No, that is not true.

If it didn't matter to God that you take time out of your week to give Him praise and honor, then He would not have made it one of the top ten in his seminar on moral basics.

The sentence for breaking this Commandment is the same as for the first three – death.

THE FIFTH COMMANDMENT:

Honor your father and your mother, that your days may be long upon the land which the LORD your God is giving you.
(Deuteronomy 5:16, KJV)

Have you always honored your parents in a way that was pleasing in the sight of God?

Have you always honored others placed in authority over you?

Ask God to remind you of the sins of your youth. You may have forgotten those sins, but God hasn't.

Steven's father and mother did some things wrong, yet they raised him the best they knew how with what they had to work with. But Steven never honored them as a dope fiend who was stealing from them, thus, sinning against this Commandment, a commandment fundamental to our society. If there isn't respect for parents, then there will not be respect for teachers, or policemen, or the laws, or for city and federal governments.

In essence, the foundational aspects of our society start to fall apart. God knew that honoring our parents was fundamental to the family, and that respect and honor to other authorities was foundational to the success of any nation.

Even as Christians, we are challenged to honor our appointed leaders – our pastors, our priests, our bishops – because God understood that without respect for both civil and spiritual authority, there will be chaos.

The sentence for breaking this Commandment is death.

THE SIXTH COMMANDMENT:

Thou shalt not kill.
(Deuteronomy 5:17, KJV)

So many feel that they are off the hook on this one. "Well, at least I've never murdered anyone."

Unfortunately, it isn't that black and white.

All murder stems from anger and hatred. Before one can murder, one must possess the attitude of murder. Can any of us ever say that we never hated someone else?

Jesus warned that if you get angry, you are in danger of judgment. Scripture speaks about the wrath of a parent "killing" the spirit of a child.

The Bible tells us that if you harbor hate in your heart for another, then in God's eyes, that is the same as murder. If you "think" about wanting to murder someone, you are guilty of murder.

You see, you can violate God's Law by attitude and by intent, as well as action. That's why Scripture tells us that if a man thinks lustful thoughts in his heart, he is guilty of adultery.

this Commandment also includes having a deep respect for human life, respect for the dignity of persons, and the constant safeguarding of peace.

How many legal abortions have been committed in this nation? We understand it is now over 2 million!

That's real, literal murder.

How many wives have been beaten by their husbands?

How many daughters have been abused by their fathers?

How many children have been needlessly beaten by angry parents?

All of these actions fall under this Commandment, and the sentence for breaking this Commandment is death.

THE SEVENTH COMMANDMENT:

Neither shalt thou commit adultery.
(Deuteronomy 5:18, KJV)

Who of us can say that we are pure of heart?

Jesus warned:

> *You have heard that it was said to those of old, you shall not commit adultery. But I say to you, that whoever looks at a woman to lust after her, has committed adultery already with her in his heart.*
(Matthew 5:27-28, KJV)

Remember, God has seen every thought, and knows about every sin you have ever committed. The day will come when you will have to face His moral law in judgment.

The Bible tells us that the impure, the fornicators, those who have had sex before marriage, and adulterers will not enter the Kingdom of God unless they accept Jesus and repednt of their sins.

Clearly, the punishment for a transgression of this Commandment is the death penalty.

THE EIGHTH COMMANDMENT:

Neither shalt thou steal.

(Deuteronomy 5:19, KJV)

Have you ever taken something that belonged to someone else, irrespective of its value? If you have, you are a thief and cannot enter God's Kingdom.

This Commandment concerns the private ownership of goods, and the respect for the goods of others.

Imagine the chaos in any society that did not observe this law. Fences could not be built high enough. Locks could not be built strong enough. The police force would never be large enough to maintain order in the midst of a people dedicated to taking the goods of others.

"But I only take a few pencils from work."

That's stealing. Even if the company you work for is Microsoft, and they have 23 billion dollars in the bank, you still do not have the right to take property that does not belong to you.

Stealing has nothing to do with whether the person you take from will suffer from the loss. It has everything to do with you walking in a moral law that demonstrates that you follow God's standard.

"But I only take a few extra tax deductions on my yearly returns. It doesn't hurt the IRS any."

That's stealing, and God forbids it, even if the IRS never notices it.

"I know my kid is thirteen, but we get a discount at the movie theater when I tell them she is twelve."

That's stealing, and you are teaching your precious young daughter to also learn how to lie.

The sentence for breaking this Commandment is death.

THE NINTH COMMANDMENT

Neither shalt thou bear false witness against thy neighbour.

(Deuteronomy 5:20, KJV)

Have you ever told a lie?

Then, you are a liar.

How many lies do you have to tell to be a liar?

Just one.

The Bible warns that all liars will have their part in the lake of fire and brimstone. You may not think that deceitfulness is a serious sin, but God thinks it is a very serious sin.

The penalty for breaking this Commandment is death.

THE TENTH COMMANDMENT

Neither shalt thou desire thy neighbour's wife, neither shalt thou covet thy neighbour's house, his field, or his manservant, or his maid-servant, his ox, or his ass, or any thing that is thy neighbour's [husband–author's addition].
(Deuteronomy 5:21, KJV)

Adultery and fornication begin in the mind.

You see your neighbor out working in the yard and start to fantasize about them in an adulterous manner.

You see a co-worker in the coffee lounge and wonder how that person would be in a romantic interlude.

This sin is the root of every adulterous affair, every sin of fornication, every sin of homosexuality.

This Commandment protects you from fantasy about your neighbor, which ultimately can lead to actions.

The sentence for breaking this Commandment is death.

Do not covet your neighbor's goods.

Do not passionately desire anything that belongs to another person. Those who covet will not inherit the Kingdom. Our desire to covet causes social disorder, poverty of the heart, and disruption within our fragile society.

The sentence for breaking all of these Commandments is death.

When we examine God's standard, His moral law, most of us have ten out of ten death sentences!!! Most of us have broken every single Commandment and we have earned ten death sentences.

Yet, one sin can send you to hell.

James said,

> *For whoever shall keep the whole law, and yet stumble in one point, he is guilty of all.*
> (James 2:10, NKJV)

When you stand before God on Judgment Day, if your sin has not been cleansed and forgiven through the blood of Jesus Christ, with God as your Judge rather than your Savior, He will say,

"You are a covetous, lying, thieving, adulterer, a murderer, one who dishonors your parents, a Sabbath breaker, blasphemer, an idolater who has put other gods before Me. How do you plead?"

The law stops our mouth!!!

All have sinned and come up short of His Law.

THE CRIMINAL LAW PARALLELS THE SPIRITUAL LAW

As a retired lawman, Rocky understands this principle better than most; he knows how the law works.

He understands what it means to be in court and see the judge pronounce the sentence. He understands the presenting of evidence through testimonies and affidavits against the people he has arrested.

Frequently, when one of his arrests would go to court, the accused would say, "Your honor, it is true that Detective Flowers caught me doing such and such, but up until that time I had a perfect record."

Well, the law is absolute.

So, too, God's moral law is absolute.

In criminal law, the defendant has an attorney who would do anything in his power to get his client out of jail. It was Rocky's responsibility to not only defend the arrest, but also to give testimony in court against the criminal.

Part of the tools of the trade that defense attorneys use is to try and make the jurors think that the officer who effected the arrest is not credible, and that the facts are not what the officer says they are.

God's moral law, through the Ten Commandments, is just and true; there is no disputing them.

In a criminal courtroom the judge does not allow "hearsay," but defense attorneys always try to introduce it in an attempt to sway the jurors because credibility is always an issue. In the courts, there was no way for Rocky to effectively prove that he was a true, honest law enforcement officer. There were so many factors, such as paperwork, experience, how articulate you were to present the facts of the case, how the officer came by the arrest of the individual.

Plus, there were other factors you could not account for, such as the craftiness of the defense attorney.

But, God's laws are true and cannot be disputed!

Man's laws are twisted and are constantly changing according to the culture, according to standards set forth not only by our legislatures, but also by how the laws are interpreted by our judges. Many times, a court will hand down a ruling that goes against all the officer knows, and against all the rulings previously handed down by our forefathers. (If you research American history, you will learn that our laws were originally founded on the Ten Commandments.)

In the courtroom, the factor that determines whether or not a person is guilty is credibility. The guilt or innocence depends on whether or not the jurors believe what has been presented to them. In the midst of the many overwhelming factors that determine a person's guilt, it all rests on man's interpretation, on man's views, and not on God's moral laws as handed down by the Ten Commandments.

Romans 2:15, KJV speaks of this:

Which shew the work of the law written in their hearts, their conscience also bearing witness, and their thoughts the mean while accusing or else excusing one another;

There is a contrast between man's criminal laws, which are corrupted, twisted, and perverted, and God's moral law from which our criminal laws come.

God's laws are straight like an arrow, and they should always be used to make all moral judgments. There is no such thing in God's courtroom about being guilty beyond a reasonable doubt.

There is no doubt!!!

When we stand before the bar of Heaven, we are guilty of breaking all of God's commandments and deserve to go to Hell. The Bible clearly says that at that Great White Throne Judgment, the books will be opened, and things written in those books will be read. If your name is not found written in The Book of Life, you will be cast into the lake that burns with fire and brimstone. You will experience an eternal incarceration in God's penitentiary called "The Lake of Fire."

There will be no appeal bond or parole date.

It is over!!!

No probation, no fines.

Your punishment will be eternal, based on breaking just one commandment which would bring one death sentence which is eternal.

Part Three

Undeserved,
Unmerited
Grace

CHAPTER TWELVE

Who Hasn't Sinned?

Who among us can say that we are not guilty of breaking all these Commandments?

All of us have sinned. The Bible warns that whoever shall keep the whole law and yet stumble in just one point is guilty of breaking all of the moral law. We'd like to share a simple story to illustrate man's standard versus God's view of our sinful lives.

Once upon a time, a little girl was watching a sheep eat grass. She thought, "That sheep sure looks bright white against the green background of the grass." No sooner had she spoken these words than it began to snow. Suddenly she thought, "That sheep sure looks dirty against the pure white snow."

In both instances, the little girl still saw the same sheep, but against a different background.

When we compare ourselves to the background of man's standards, we look pretty clean. But when we compare ourselves to the pure, snow white righteousness of God's standard, which is the moral law, then we see ourselves in truth, and know that we are unclean in His sight.

God's Law is the holy standard by which all humanity will be judged on Judgment Day.

STOP TRYING

This may sound strange, but the worst thing you can do if the Holy Spirit is convicting you that you have lived a sinful lifestyle is "to try" and clean up your life. It is good that you realize you have sinned, and that you are determined, from now on, to try and keep the Ten Commandments, to do good deeds, to say the right things, and to think only pure thoughts.

But should a judge let a murderer go just because the murderer says he will not do it again, and is now determined to live a good life?

Of course not!

The murderer owes a debt to society and must be punished for the murder he has already committed.

God's Law acts like a mirror, showing you the truth. If you see egg on your face, you do not try and wash yourself with the mirror. The purpose of the mirror is to send you to the water for cleansing.

Neither should you try and wash yourself with the mirror of God's Law. That is not its purpose. The sight in the mirror is not a pretty one, but if you do not face it and acknowledge that you are unclean, then all that dirt will be presented on Judgment Day as evidence of your guilt.

Then, it will be too late to be cleansed.

"GOD WILL OVERLOOK IT."

Perhaps you think that God is good, and so He will overlook your sins.

If you are guilty of a terrible crime in a criminal court, and you admit to the judge that you are guilty of the crime, can you then say, "But judge, I know you are a good man and will overlook my crimes?"

The judge would probably respond by saying, "You are right, I am a good man, and because of my goodness, I am going to see that justice is done in this court and that you are punished for your crimes."

The very thing many people hope will save them on Judgment Day is God's "goodness" – the very thing that will condemn them. If God is good (and He is), He will punish murderers, liars, thieves, adulterers, fornicators, and homosexuals. Hell will be their dreadful fate.

If you read in the newspaper that a man received a $5.00 fine for a crime, you would conclude that his crime was insignificant. But if a man received multiple life sentences, you would conclude that his crime was heinous. In the same way, we can catch a glimpse

of how terrible sin must be in the sight of God by looking to the punishment given for sin – eternal damna-
tion.

JUST PUNISHMENT

Ungrateful humanity seldom bothers to thank
God for His wonderful blessings of color, light, food,
joy, beauty, love, and laughter. Because of our ingrat-
itude, God should take those blessings away from
them. Instead of proving our gratitude by obedience
to His will, we use His name as a curse word.

Our punishment will be just and severe to the
uttermost – an eternity in Hell.

Here's what Jesus said Hell was like.

*And if thy hand offend thee, cut it off: it is
better for thee to enter into life maimed, than
having two hands to go into hell, into the fire
that never shall be quenched: Where their
worm dieth not, and the fire is not quenched.
And if thy foot offend thee, cut it off: it is better
for thee to enter halt into life, than having two
feet to be cast into hell, into the fire that never
shall be quenched: Where their worm dieth
not, and the fire is not quenched. And if thine
eye offend thee, pluck it out: it is better for thee
to enter into the kingdom of God with one eye,
than having two eyes to be cast into hell fire:
Where their worm dieth not, and the fire is not
quenched.*

(Mark 9:43-48, KJV)

Please, look honestly into the mirror of God's moral law; then seek the water that cleanses every sin. If you do not believe what we are saying about the reality of Hell, it means you think God is corrupt, that He does not have the moral backbone to seek justice, that Jesus was a liar, and that the apostles were false witnesses.

If you believe that God's promises are nothing but prefabricated lies, then you are giving no greater insult to God than to call Him a liar. By doing so, you are adding to your transgressions.

Imagine, if you reject the Savior, die in your sins, and find that what we have written here is the truth, then it will be too late for you.

You will be judged for your sins.

If that happens, and your eyes meet our eyes on the Day of Judgment, we are free from your blood. We have told you the truth, but you have chosen to ignore it; your blood will be on your own head; you will have no one to blame but yourself.

Can you see your predicament? You are guilty of sinning against God Himself. And because you have a conscience, you have sinned with knowledge.

JUSTICE SERVED

Isn't it true that every time you lied, lusted, etc., you did it with the full knowledge that it was wrong?

Does the fact that you have sinned against God scare you?

It should.

You have actually angered Him by your sin. The Bible says,

> *And you, who once were alienated and enemies in your mind by wicked works, yet now He has reconciled.*
>
> (Colossians 1:21, NKJV)

Let fear work for your good in the same way that the fear of jumping out of an airplane at a great height would make you put on a parachute. Let your will to live open your heart to the Gospel of salvation.

God does not want you to perish.

> *That whosoever believeth in him should not perish, but have eternal life.*
>
> (John 3:15, KJV)

To make it clear what an incredible thing He has done for you in the Gospel, let us look again to the criminal law.

Imagine that you are standing in front of a judge, guilty of very serious crimes. All the evidence has been presented, and there is no doubt about your guilt. The fine for your crime is $250,000 or imprisonment, but you do not have two pennies to rub together. As the judge is about to pass sentence, lifting up his gavel, someone you do not even know steps into the courtroom and pays the fine for you.

The moment you accept that payment you are free to go.

Justice has been served; the law has been satisfied.

The stranger who paid your fine has demonstrated how much he cares for you.

His payment was evidence of his love.

That is what God did for you in the person of Jesus Christ!

You are guilty, but He paid the fine 2000 years ago! The Bible puts it this way:

> *But He was wounded for our transgressions, He was bruised for our guilt and iniquities; the chastisement [needful to obtain] peace and well-being for us was upon Him, and with the stripes [that wounded] Him we are healed and made whole.*
>
> (Isaiah 53:5, AMP)

Christ has redeemed us from the curse of the law, being made a curse for us. God commended His love toward us in that while we were yet sinners, Christ died for us. It was no small thing for Jesus to die for us. The only thing that would satisfy the demands of the eternal law was the suffering and death of the sinless Son of God.

How To Approach God

What love God has for you! He suffered unspeakable agony so that you would not need to be punished for your sins. His sacrificial death and resurrection mean that you no longer need to be in debt to the moral law.

God gave you His grace so you can now experience everlasting life if you obey Him.

Death no longer has a legal hold upon those who belong to Christ Jesus. Let us share another story to help illustrate this vital spiritual truth.

Two men were offered a parachute while sitting in an airplane. The first man was told that the parachute would improve his flight, but the second man was told that he had to make a 25,000 foot jump. When the flight struck severe turbulence, the first man took his parachute off because, as far as he was concerned, it did not improve his flight. But during that same, violent turbulence, the second man clung tighter to his parachute. Each man's motive for putting his parachute on determined whether or not he would keep it on.

In the same way, you should not put on the Lord Jesus Christ just to find peace, joy, true happiness, to have your marriage healed, or your problems fixed: in other words, to have your flight improved.

You put on the Lord Jesus Christ to escape the

jump to come. You know you are going to pass through the door of death. So, when the flight gets bumpy, when problems come, you will not fall away from the faith.

Repent and put your trust in Jesus Christ as your Lord and Savior. Do not put it off until tomorrow. Would you sell an eye for a million dollars? How about both eyes for twenty million?

Of course not!

No one in his right mind would sell his eyes; they are priceless.

Yet, your eyes are merely the windows to your soul. Your light, your soul is of such value that Jesus said that you should despise the value of your eyes compared to your soul. He said,

> *And if thy right eye offend thee, pluck it out, and cast it from thee: for it is profitable for thee that one of thy members should perish, and not that thy whole body should be cast into hell.*
> (Matthew 5:29, KJV)

In other words, of all the things that you should prioritize in your life, it is not your health, your vocation, your family, your money...it is your eternal salvation.

Think of a man who has committed adultery. His faithful wife is more than willing to take him back. So what is the attitude in which he should approach her?

It should be out of tremendous humility, asking her for forgiveness, and determining in his heart never to even think of committing adultery again.

That is how you should approach God!

If you are not sure how to pray, read Psalms 51 and make it your prayer. Then put your faith in Jesus Christ the same way you would put your faith in a parachute: You do more than believe it will benefit you; you actually trust yourself to it by putting it on.

Once you have made your peace with God, read the Bible daily and obey what you have read.

Remember, the Ten Commandments are the blue-print God handed down for us to follow and believe. But, they are just the beginning. If we cannot adhere to the beginning, then there is no way we are going to be able to make it at the end.

If we break any of the Commandments, we have sinned and deserve death.

But, when you give your life to Christ, His sentence for you will be life, not death.

For all of us, the death sentence has already been handed down because of our sin. The only way that death sentence can be overturned is to surrender your life to the Lordship of Jesus Christ. He does not just suspend your sentence, He exonerates you and releases you of all past sin.

Receive Romans 3:23 into your life.

For all have sinned, and come short of the glory of God.

(Romans 3:23, KJV)

All of us have broken the Commandments. Before we knew Him, we all had other gods before Him. For all of us, until we come to accept Jesus as Lord and Savior, the God of the Bible is not first in our lives.

CHAPTER THIRTEEN

The Saving Grace of Forgiveness

True repentance leads to Godly grief which leads to salvation. Godly repentance leads and contributes to salvation and deliverance from evil; it never brings regret. This change of heart leads to a change of mind which leads to a change of lifestyle that brings the saving grace of forgiveness.

When Steven was in that mental hospital, with no way of knowing if he was ever going to come out, there was a peace that passed over all his understanding and soul, and he knew that things would be all right.

He felt washed, clean, and forgiven.

It was the sweet, saving grace of forgiveness because he had truly repented; the Holy Spirit had convicted him of his sin. He began to understand the weight of God's holiness, of God's true standard of right and wrong, understanding that no human being could ever obtain absolute perfection.

You Cannot Meet the Standard

When a person says, "I keep the Ten Commandments," they are immediately breaking one of them because they are lying.

No one has kept the Ten Commandments except Jesus Christ.

God set the standard and we cannot keep it; the standard was never given to us to keep. The standard was given to show us that we cannot keep it.

That fact drives us to our Savior.

That is why the book of Galatians teaches that the Law is a tutor, a schoolmaster, designed to lead us to Jesus Christ.

> *[21]Is the law then against the promises of God? God forbid: for if there had been a law given which could have given life, verily righteousness should have been by the law.*
>
> *[22]But the scripture hath concluded all under sin, that the promise by faith of Jesus Christ might be given to them that believe.*
>
> *[23]But before faith came, we were kept under the law, shut up unto the faith which should afterwards be revealed.*
> (Galatians 3:21-23, KJV)

Paul is speaking to the church in Galatia which was a very legalistic church. He essentially states, "Is the law then contrary and opposed to the promises of

God? Of course not. For if the law had been given which could confer spiritual light, then righteousness and right standing with God would certainly have come by law."

Scripture depicts all mankind as shut up and imprisoned by sin. Why? So the inheritance, the blessing which was promised through faith in Jesus Christ, the Messiah, might be given, released, delivered, and committed to all those who believe, who adhere to, who trust, in and fully rely on Him!

We were once perpetually guarded under the law, kept in custody in preparation for the faith which was destined to be revealed, unveiled, and disclosed. The Law served as our trainer, our guardian, our guide to Christ to lead us, until Christ came. Only then were we justified, declared righteous, put in right standing with God by a true faith.

Now that faith has come, we are no longer under a trainer, the guardian of our childhood. For in Christ Jesus we are all sons of God through faith.

For as we are baptized into a spiritual union and communion with Christ, the Anointed One, the Messiah, we are then clothed in Him.

It makes no difference if you are Jew or Greek, black or white, male or female, we are all one in Christ Jesus, and spiritual heirs according to the promise.

The Law was given to us as a schoolmaster, as a tutor to bring us to Christ. Once faith in Christ comes, we are no longer under the schoolmaster. We are released from the custody of the law through and by our faith in Jesus Christ.

LAW AND GRACE

The law and grace are like heads and tails on a coin: they are both needed. We must preach the law of God's Ten Commandments to convict the sinner that we are all sinners in need of rescue.

[7]What shall we say then? Is the law sin? God forbid. Nay, I had not known sin, but by the law: for I had not known lust, except the law had said, Thou shalt not covet.

[8]But sin, taking occasion by the commandment, wrought in me all manner of concupiscence. For without the law sin was dead.

[9]For I was alive without the law once: but when the commandment came, sin revived, and I died.

[10]And the commandment, which was ordained to life, I found to be unto death.

[11]For sin, taking occasion by the commandment, deceived me, and by it slew me.

[12]Wherefore the law is holy, and the commandment holy, and just, and good.

[13]Was then that which is good made death unto me? God forbid. But sin, that it might appear

sin, working death in me by that which is good; that sin by the commandment might become exceeding sinful.
(Romans 7:7-13, KJV)

Paul essentially says, "What then do we conclude? Is the law identical with sin?"

Certainly not, nevertheless, if it had not been for the Law, we would not recognize sin or know its meaning. For instance, we would not know about coveting if we did not have a conscious awareness of that sin. The Law repeatedly said "You shall not covet or have an evil desire for another's wife or goods."

The Law is holy (verse 12) and so each Commandment is holy, just, and good. The Commandments pinpoint sin, and the Law makes the immeasurable sinfulness of sin plainly appear.

The Law of Moses (the Ten Commandments) was given by God through Moses in the Old Testament to show us that every human being is a sinner, deserving eternal judgment and death.

No one has kept the Ten Commandments; no one has obeyed God's Law.

The only way to be saved is by trusting in the only One who did keep the Law, which was God Himself, through His Son.

That is where law and grace kiss!

YES, YOU ARE INDEED A SINNER

Many preach what we call "the Gospel of easy believism" which is just telling people that "Jesus loves you and has died for your sins." That is true, but the problem with that simple preaching is that people in our western culture do not believe that they are sinners.

We say things like, "I'm not like those fellows in the state penitentiary. I'm not like them. I'm not a sinner; I'm a good person."

We all are sinners until we acknowledge that God and His grace is something we cannot begin to fathom.

Before you give your life to Christ, it is impossible to fathom God's grace.

Grace is God's unmerited favor; in reality, we all deserve death.

God's Law does not care if you are rich or poor, nor does it care where you come from, or evaluate how much education, or how many degrees you have. All of those things mean absolutely nothing.

We thank God for His grace that leads to repentance and ultimately to salvation. We cannot reason our way out of sin, nor buy our way out.

It is only by His grace.

Paul, rebuking the Jews in Romans 2:17-24 KJV, said:

¹⁷Behold, thou art called a Jew, and rest in the law, and makest thy boast of God,

¹⁸And knowest his will, and approvest the things that are more excellent, being instructed out of the law;

¹⁹And art confident that thou thyself art a guide of the blind, a light of them which are in darkness,

²⁰An instructor of the foolish, a teacher of babes, which hast the form of knowledge and of the truth in the law.

²¹Thou therefore which teachest another, teachest thou not thyself? thou that preachest a man should not steal, dost thou steal?

²²Thou that sayest a man should not commit adultery, dost thou commit adultery? Thou that abhorrest idols, dost thou commit sacrilege?

²³Thou that makest thy boast of the law, through breaking the law dishonourest thou God?

²⁴For the name of God is blasphemed among the Gentiles through you, as it is written.

The Amplified Bible puts it this way:

But if you bear the name of Jew, and rely upon the law and pride yourself in God and your relationship to Him, and know and understand

His will and discerningly approve the better things, and have a sense of what is vital because you are instructed by the law, and if you are confident that you, yourself are a guide to the blind and a light to those who are in darkness and you are a corrector of the foolish and a teacher of the childish, having in the law the embodiment of knowledge and truth well then, you teach others, do you not teach yourself? While you teach against stealing, do you steal? Take that which does not belong to you? (one of the commandments) You who say not to commit adultery, do you commit adultery? (seventh commandment) Are you unchaste in your action or in your thought? You who abhor and loathe idols, do you rob temples, do you appropriate to your own use that which is consecrated to God and thus do it sacrilege? Do you who boast in the law, do you dishonor God by breaking the law, by infringing upon and carelessly neglecting or openly breaking it? For it is written the name of God is maligned and blasphemed among the gentiles because of you.

Every time God mentions the Law, He is referring back to the moral law, the Ten Commandments. That is the reason WHY Satan has worked successfully to get the moral law of God out of the hearts, minds, awareness, and consciousness of the people in this nation. He effectively got rid of Jesus Christ being God and Savior. He eliminated prayer, the Ten Commandments, and the Bible, the foundational pillars of Christian faith and belief.

That is why America is on a collision course with God. It is only by the grace and mercy of God that we have not been consumed.

SAVING GRACE

Understand the saving grace of forgiveness.

We are forgiven even though we have broken every one of the Ten Commandments. God saved us. He knew we could not keep His Commandments no matter how badly we wanted to keep them.

God, in His grace and mercy, covered us all with His Blood.

The Bible says that,

> *If we confess our sins, He is faithful and just to forgive us our sins, and cleanse us from all unrighteousness.*
>
> (1 John 1:9, KJV)

That is the saving grace of forgiveness!

That repentance, that changed heart, leads to a changed mind that leads to a changed lifestyle. Repentance comes through grace that leads to salvation and deliverance from evil.

Like-minded and like-spirited men and women can come together in one accord and have a sweet friendship and fellowship, one with the other, because we are born of God and the Kingdom of God.

We have collectively experienced the forgiveness of our sins.

CHAPTER FOURTEEN

Where Is the Unity?

Why do Christians battle each other?

We don't know.

The only answer that we have been able to come up with that satisfies us both spiritually and intellectually is the fact that many who claim to be Christians (and the Bible bears this out) are not really changed Christians at all.

They have never been changed in their hearts, resulting in a change in their thinking about their brothers and sisters.

> *...He who hateth his brother abideth in death.*
> (1 John 3:14, KJV)

You see, there are many who have never changed their hearts. Their minds have not been changed, and their lifestyles have not been changed.

CHRISTIAN ONENESS

It is an embarrassment when the world can stand up and say that "We treat our own better than the church treats their people."

So, there is a problem when we have so-called "Christians" battling each other while we watch the world around us sink into sin, going to Hell.

Our oneness is exemplified when Christians worship together in a union most people cannot begin to understand. It goes beyond boundaries of race, creed, color, status in life, rich, poor, etc.

Worship is a form a fellowship you cannot begin to describe to someone who is not a Christian.

WHERE IS THE FELLOWSHIP?

Rocky served in various units in the New York City Police Department where the numbers were small, yet, these units still encountered strife, anger, and a slew of other problems in their personal relationships with each other. He understood that dissension was part of our human nature, yet, in his spirit these negative encounters deeply grieved him.

"Here we are, serving the people of New York City," he'd think, "protecting life and property, but yet fellowship between us is almost void." The only fellowship that did seem to occur was at the local watering hole – a bar – or at some other kind of activity involving alcoholic consumption.

Fellowship at the local watering hole (a bar) is a falsehood fueled by liquor. The more alcohol consumed, the more cutting and stabbing take place. Rocky would frequently wonder, "If that lieutenant over there is cutting up his former captain, I can only imagine what he's saying about his subordinates down the hallway."

Jesus said,

Brood of vipers! How can you, being evil, speak good things? For out of the abundance of the heart the mouth speaks.

(Matthew 12:34, NKJV)

Many try and justify what they say when they are drunk. "Oh, that's not me, that's just the liquor talking."

No, that was you talking because liquor cannot talk. Alcohol stirs up what is in your heart and brings it out of your mouth.

The only place where you will ever encounter true fellowship is in the Body of Christ.

That fellowship can be deeper than what you experience in your own family, or in your childhood friendships. The best fellowship is in the Body of Christ when the hearts have been transformed and changed by God's grace.

Some of you reading this book might ask one of these tough and penetrating questions:

"If there is fellowship among Christians, then why are Christians the only ones to shoot their wounded?"

"Why were Christians the slave-masters during the foundation of this country?"

"Why were Christians the murdering crusaders during the Inquisition?"

The answer to all of those questions is the same:

Those folks had "a form of godliness, but they denied the power thereof."

They were not really Christians because they were not following God's mandates nor being true to the One whose name they claimed, the Name of Jesus Christ.

The word "Christian" comes from the word "Christ-like" or "Christ follower."

We prefer the term "disciples."

The Bible only uses the term "Christian" one time, and then it was in a negative concept given by unbelievers at Antioch.

But, the Bible always talks about Jesus' disciples, those who were discipled and disciplined to follow Jesus Christ.

THE STRONG GRACE OF FREEDOM

The repentance experience from the grace of God leads to salvation and deliverance from evil, and it brings forth the sweet grace of fellowship, and the sweet grace of freedom.

After one year at Crenshaw Christian Center, Rev. Craft got married in that church.

As a direct result of the sweet grace of true Christian fellowship, and that repentance which is brought about through grace, they experienced the strong grace of freedom!

They knew beyond a shadow of a doubt that they were forgiven, that they had wonderful fellowship, and that they had freedom from their sins.

CHAPTER FIFTEEN

A Short Epilogue

Now that you have completed *Virtue and Vice*, Rocky and I are wondering if you are starting to recognize some very important things about your own life.

Have you been living in depression for so long that you have wondered if it wasn't triggered by a chemical imbalance?

Have you been contemplating suicide, even though on the surface your life doesn't really seem that bad?

Are you leading a "double life," acting one way around your family and friends, but living in sin behind their backs, thinking no one knows?

Do you feel you have done a great job of hiding the hideous sins that are rapidly becoming a seemingly permanent part of your nature?

Do you feel in bondage to your sins, convinced that there is no way out?

Friend, in our experience, so much of depression, so much of life's desperation, so much of suicide, and a sense of futility is rooted in one single cause:

SIN!

As you give your life to Christ, and follow the pattern we have discussed in this humble book, amazing things will happen.

Severe depression will be replaced with incredible and lasting joy.

Suicide and a sense of futility will be replaced by a meaningful life.

Your double life will be replaced by a life uniquely and totally dedicated to one purpose: developing a personal relationship with your Lord, Savior and Messiah, Jesus Christ.

Your hiding will stop. Instead, you will become a light to all who know you.

Your bondage will be broken, and for the first time in your life, you will be truly free.

Don't wait.

Repent.

Follow the path to virtue.

Allow God's grace to transform you.

ABOUT THE AUTHORS

Reverend Steven L. Craft is the executive Director of Christian Citizenship Ministries, Inc. He was a former Correctional Chaplain at the Missouri State Penitentiary, in Jefferson City, Missouri. He is ordained and endorsed with the American Baptist Churches, U.S.A. Reverend Craft holds a Bachelor's of Arts from Central Bible College, in Springfield, Missouri, and a Master of Divinity from Harvard Divinity School, in Cambridge, Massachusetts. He is a Doctoral Candidate at Eastern Baptist Theological Seminary, in Philadelphia, Pennsylvania.

Retired Detective Roxon Flowers is the treasurer for Christian Citizenship Ministries, Inc. He worked in various units within the New York City Police Department, and concluded his law enforcement career in the Vice Enforcement Division. Detective Flowers holds a degree from the City University of New York in Elementary Education. He has completed numerous courses in Criminal Justice throughout his twenty years with the New York City Police Department. He has committed his life to sharing his story of God's mercy and grace in a dangerous and violent criminal environment on the streets of New York City.